PANINI PRESS COOKBOOK

PANINI PRESS RECIPES FOR ALL TYPES OF DELICIOUS PANINI'S

By
BookSumo Press
Copyright © by Saxonberg Associates

Published by
BookSumo Press, a DBA of Saxonberg Associates
http://www.booksumo.com/

TABLE OF CONTENTS

ANY ISSUES? CONTACT US

If you find that something important to you is missing from this book please contact us at info@booksumo.com.

We will take your concerns into consideration when the 2nd edition of this book is published. And we will keep you updated!

— BookSumo Press

LEGAL NOTES

COMMON ABBREVIATIONS

cup(s)	C.
tablespoon	tbsp
teaspoon	tsp
ounce	oz.
pound	lb.

*All units used are standard American measurements

CHAPTER 1: EASY PANINI RECIPES

BAJA TUNA PANINI

Ingredients

- 2 (6 oz.) cans tuna, drained
- 2 tbsp light mayonnaise
- 2 tbsp plain yogurt
- 1/2 roasted red pepper, diced
- 1/4 C. celery, diced
- 2 green onions, chopped
- 3 marinated artichokes, hearts chopped
- salt and pepper
- 4 Italian rolls, halved horizontally
- 4 slices provolone cheese

Directions

- In a bowl, add all the ingredients except the rolls and cheese and mix until well combined.
- Place the tuna mixture onto the bottom half of each bun evenly, followed by the cheese.
- Cover each with the top half of the buns.
- Place a grill pan over medium heat until heated through.
- Add the sandwiches and cook for about 5 minutes, flipping once half way through and pressing often with the back of a spoon.
- Enjoy warm.

Servings Per Recipe: 4

Timing Information:

Preparation	15 mins
Total Time	20 mins

Nutritional Information:

Calories	403.9
Fat	16.1g
Cholesterol	55.2mg
Sodium	877.3mg
Carbohydrates	31.4g
Protein	33.8g

* Percent Daily Values are based on a 2,000 calorie diet.

FLORIDA CHICKEN PANINI

Ingredients

- 4 boneless skinless chicken breasts, pounded
- 3 tbsp olive oil
- 1 tbsp minced garlic
- 1 tbsp dried Italian seasoning
- salt and pepper

- 1 1/2 C. roasted red peppers
- 4 slices provolone cheese
- 1/2-3/4 C. pesto sauce
- 8 slices Italian bread
- olive oil

Directions

- Arrange the chicken breasts between 2 sheets of wax paper and with a meat mallet, pound into an even thickness.
- In a bowl, add the garlic, 3 tbsp of the oil, Italian seasoning and pepper and mix well. Add the chicken breasts and coat with the oil mixture generously. Place in the fridge for about 2 hours.
- Remove the chicken breasts from the marinade and sprinkle with the salt and pepper evenly. Place a skillet over medium heat until heated through. Add the chicken pieces and cook for about 10 minutes, flipping once half way through. Transfer the chicken breasts onto a plate. Place the roasted peppers over each chicken breast evenly, followed by 1 cheese slice. Place the pesto onto both sides of each bread slice evenly. Place 1 chicken breast onto each of 4 bread slices. Cover with the remaining bread slices.
- Coat the outsides of each sandwich with olive oil.
- Place a grill pan over medium-high heat until heated through.
- Place 2 panini sandwiches and top with another heavy skillet for weight, followed by a heavy can.
- Cook for about 6 minutes, flipping once half way through.
- Repeat with the remaining sandwiches.
- Cut each sandwich in half and enjoy.

Servings Per Recipe: 4

Timing Information:

Preparation	1 hr 30 mins
Total Time	1 hr 30 mins

Nutritional Information:

Calories	443.2
Fat	22.2g
Cholesterol	94.8mg
Sodium	1335.0mg
Carbohydrates	23.3g
Protein	36.2g

* Percent Daily Values are based on a 2,000 calorie diet.

Asiago Panini Toscano

Ingredients

- 1/2 C. shredded fresh mozzarella cheese
- 1/2 C. shredded Fontina cheese
- 3 tbsp asiago cheese, grated
- 1/2 C. shredded provolone cheese
- 8 slices tomatoes, sliced
- 1 tbsp basil, chopped
- 4 ciabatta rolls, halved lengthwise
- 8 arugula leaves

Directions

- In a bowl, add all the cheeses and mix well.
- Place the cheese mixture onto the bottom half of each roll, followed by the tomato slices.
- Drizzle with the oil and top with the basil, followed by the arugula leaves.
- Cover each with the top halve of the buns.
- Place a cast-iron skillet over medium-high heat until heated through.
- Place the panini in skillet and top with another heavy skillet for weight.
- Cook for about 6 minutes, flipping once half way through.
- Cut the panini in half and enjoy.

Servings Per Recipe: 4

Timing Information:

Preparation	10 mins
Total Time	16 mins

Nutritional Information:

Calories	160.8
Fat	11.8g
Cholesterol	38.1mg
Sodium	343.4mg
Carbohydrates	2.6g
Protein	11.2g

* Percent Daily Values are based on a 2,000 calorie diet.

German Chocolate Panini

Ingredients

- 4 -6 oz. semisweet chocolate, chopped
- 2 tbsp butter, melted
- 8 slices bread, thick
- icing sugar

Directions

- Place the butter onto one side of all bread slices evenly.
- Arrange 4 bread slices onto a platter, buttered side down.
- Place the chocolate onto each of 4 slices about 1/4-inch from the crust.
- Top with the remaining bread slices, buttered side up.
- Place a nonstick skillet over medium-low heat until heated through.
- Place 2 panini sandwiches and cook for about 3-4 minutes per side, pressing with a spatula frequently.
- Repeat with the remaining sandwiches.
- Cut each sandwich in half and enjoy warm with a dusting of the icing sugar.

Servings Per Recipe: 4

Timing Information:

Preparation	10 mins
Total Time	26 mins

Nutritional Information:

Calories	329.2
Fat	22.5g
Cholesterol	15.2mg
Sodium	313.1mg
Carbohydrates	33.9g
Protein	7.6g

* Percent Daily Values are based on a 2,000 calorie diet.

PICNIC PANINI

Ingredients

- 4 slices eggplants
- extra virgin olive oil
- salt and pepper
- 8 slices country sliced bread
- 2 C. arugula leaves
- 8 oz. sliced mozzarella cheese

Directions

- Coat the eggplant slices with the oil evenly.
- Place the grill pan over medium heat until heated through.
- Add the eggplant slices and cook for about 4 minutes. Coat the bread slices with the oil.
- Arrange 4 bread slices onto a platter, oiled side down.
- Place 1 eggplant slice over each slice, followed by arugula and mozzarella.
- Cover with the remaining 4 bread slices, oiled side up.
- In the same grill pan, place 2 sandwiches and cook, covered for about 3-4 minutes.
- Repeat with the remaining sandwiches.
- Cut each sandwich in half diagonally and enjoy.

Servings Per Recipe: 4

Timing Information:

Preparation	10 mins
Total Time	25 mins

Nutritional Information:

Calories	305.9
Fat	14.4g
Cholesterol	44.8mg
Sodium	614.3mg
Carbohydrates	26.9g
Protein	16.6g

* Percent Daily Values are based on a 2,000 calorie diet.

MOZZARELLA PROVOLONE PANINI

Ingredients

- 1/3 C. drained sun-dried tomato packed in oil, chopped
- 3 tbsp oil-cured black olives, pitted and chopped
- 1/2 tsp dried oregano
- ground pepper
- 10 slices white bread
- extra virgin olive oil
- 5 slices provolone cheese
- 1/2 lb. mozzarella cheese, sliced

Directions

- For the pesto: in a blender, add the olives, sun-dried tomatoes, oregano and pepper and pulse until a slightly chunky paste is formed.
- Coat 1 side of all the bread slices with the oil in a thin layer.
- In the bottom a baking sheet, arrange 5 bread slices, oiled side down.
- Place 1 provolone slice over 5 bread slice, followed by the tomato pesto and mozzarella cheese.
- Cover with the remaining bread slices, oiled side up.
- Place a skillet over medium-high heat until heated through.
- Place the sandwiches in batches and top with a cast-iron skillet for the weight.
- Cook for about 4 minutes, flipping once half way through.
- Cut each sandwich in half and enjoy.

Servings Per Recipe: 1

Timing Information:

| Preparation | 20 mins |
| Total Time | 30 mins |

Nutritional Information:

Calories	113.0
Fat	6.6g
Cholesterol	13.7mg
Sodium	353.2mg
Carbohydrates	8.1g
Protein	5.4g

* Percent Daily Values are based on a 2,000 calorie diet.

BASIL BEEF PANINI

Ingredients

- 8 slices Italian bread
- 2 tbsp butter, softened
- 4 tbsp prepared basil pesto
- 1/2 lb. deli roast beef, cooked, sliced
- 4 slices mozzarella cheese
- spaghetti sauce

Directions

- Place the butter onto 1 side of all the bread slices evenly.
- Place the beef over 4 bread slices evenly, followed by the pesto and cheese.
- Cover with the remaining bread slices, buttered side up.
- Place skillet over medium heat until heated through.
- Place the sandwiches, buttered side down and cook for about 4-5 minutes, flipping once half way through.
- Enjoy warm alongside the spaghetti sauce.

Servings Per Recipe: 4

Timing Information:

Preparation	15 mins
Total Time	25 mins

Nutritional Information:

Calories	322.8
Fat	15.7g
Cholesterol	65.3mg
Sodium	1102.2mg
Carbohydrates	24.2g
Protein	21.1g

* Percent Daily Values are based on a 2,000 calorie diet.

My First Panini
(Cream Cheese and Jelly)

Ingredients

- 1 loaf French bread
- cream cheese
- choice jam
- butter, melted
- powdered sugar

Directions

- Set your grill to medium-high heat.
- Cut 2 French bread slices diagonally about 1-inch thick.
- In a bowl, add the cream cheese and preserves and mix well. Spread cream cheese mixture over one side of bread slice evenly and top with remaining slice.
- Spread the bread over the outside of bread.
- Cook on grill till browned.
- Dust with the powdered sugar and serve.

Servings Per Recipe: 1

Timing Information:

Preparation	2 mins
Total Time	6 mins

Nutritional Information:

Calories	2959.3
Fat	18.7g
Cholesterol	0.0mg
Sodium	5253.1mg
Carbohydrates	577.9g
Protein	120.3g

* Percent Daily Values are based on a 2,000 calorie diet.

BRUNCH PANINI'S

Ingredients

- 8 large eggs
- 1/2 tsp kosher salt
- 1/4 tsp black pepper
- 2 tbsp unsalted butter
- 4 soft sandwich buns, halved lengthwise
- 8 oz. prosciutto, sliced, or chicken breast
- 8 oz. Swiss cheese, sliced

Directions

- In a bowl, add the eggs, pepper and salt and beat well.
- In a skillet, add 1 tbsp of the butter over medium heat and cook until heated through.
- Add the egg mixture and cook until scrambled, stirring continuously.
- Place the scrambled eggs onto the bottom half of each roll evenly, followed by the prosciutto and cheese.
- Cover each with the top of the rolls.
- In a grill pan, add the remaining butter over medium heat and cook until melted.
- Place 2 sandwiches and cook for about 2-3 minutes per side, pressing with the back of a spatula frequently.
- Repeat with the remaining 2 sandwiches.
- Enjoy warm.

Servings Per Recipe: 4

Timing Information:

Preparation	5 mins
Total Time	20 mins

Nutritional Information:

Calories	533.6
Fat	33.3g
Cholesterol	490.4mg
Sodium	673.6mg
Carbohydrates	25.1g
Protein	32.0g

* Percent Daily Values are based on a 2,000 calorie diet.

BACKYARD PANINI GRILLER

Ingredients

- 3 medium portabella mushroom caps
- 2 Vidalia onions, sliced
- 1/2 C. olive oil
- 4 garlic cloves, minced
- salt and pepper
- 1 loaf Italian bread, cut open lengthwise

Directions

- In a bowl, add the garlic, oil, salt and pepper and mix until well combined.
- Add the onions and mushrooms and coat with the mixture generously.
- Keep aside for about 25-30 minutes.
- Set your grill for medium heat and lightly, grease the grill grate.
- Cook the onions and mushrooms onto the grill over medium heat until desired doneness, coating with the oil mixture occasionally.
- Coat the bread halves with the oil evenly and onto the grill until toasted lightly.
- Place the onions and mushrooms onto the bottom portion of bread.
- Cover with the top half and press with a frying pan for some time.
- Cut into 6 equal sized portions and enjoy.

Servings Per Recipe: 4

Timing Information:

Preparation	20 mins
Total Time	35 mins

Nutritional Information:

Calories	482.2
Fat	29.9g
Cholesterol	0.0mg
Sodium	446.9mg
Carbohydrates	46.0g
Protein	8.7g

* Percent Daily Values are based on a 2,000 calorie diet.

PESTO WHOLE WHEAT PANINI

Ingredients

- 2 large beefsteak tomatoes, cored and sliced
- 1 (16 oz.) ball mozzarella cheese
- 12 slices whole wheat bread
- 1 C. pesto sauce
- kosher salt
- butter, unsalted

Directions

- Set your panini press as suggested by the manual.
- Season the tomato slices with a little salt.
- Arrange the bread slices onto a platter.
- Place the pesto onto all bread slices evenly.
- Place 1 mozzarella slice onto 6 bread slices, followed by the tomato slices.
- Sprinkle the tomato with a little salt.
- Cover with the remaining bread slices, pesto side down.
- Place the butter onto both sides of all sandwiches.
- Place the sandwiches into the panini press in batches and cook for about 2-3 minutes.
- Cut each sandwich in half and enjoy warm.

Servings Per Recipe: 6

Timing Information:

Preparation	15 mins
Total Time	18 mins

Nutritional Information:

Calories	376.4
Fat	18.9g
Cholesterol	59.8mg
Sodium	742.2mg
Carbohydrates	27.1g
Protein	24.5g

* Percent Daily Values are based on a 2,000 calorie diet.

HUBBY'S FAVORITE PANINI

Ingredients

- 2 tbsp butter, melted
- 4 slices sourdough bread
- 2 slices Swiss cheese
- 1/2 lb. deli turkey
- 1 bunch arugula, stems trimmed
- 2 tbsp raspberry jam

Directions

- Set your panini press as suggested by the manual.
- Place the butter onto one side of 2 bread slices.
- Place the jam onto remaining bread slices.
- Place the 2 bread slices into the panini press, butter sides down.
- Place the turkey onto 2 buttered bread slices, followed by the cheese and arugula.
- Cover with the remaining bread slices, jam side down.
- Now, place the butter onto the top of each sandwich.
- Cook for about 4-5 minutes.
- Enjoy warm.

Servings Per Recipe: 2

Timing Information:

Preparation	5 mins
Total Time	10 mins

Nutritional Information:

Calories	741.5
Fat	26.5g
Cholesterol	118.6mg
Sodium	2282.2mg
Carbohydrates	90.4g
Protein	34.3g

* Percent Daily Values are based on a 2,000 calorie diet.

Panini Muy Buena

Ingredients

- 1 large red bell pepper, cored, seeded and sliced
- 1/2 small red onion, peeled and sliced
- 1 tsp extra virgin olive oil
- 4 ciabatta rolls, split
- 1/4 C. garlic-infused olive oil, see appendix
- salt and pepper
- 1/2 lb. prosciutto, sliced, or salami
- 1/4 lb. provolone cheese, sliced
- 1 C. arugula
- 1 tbsp extra virgin olive oil

Directions

- In a skillet, add 1 tsp of the oil over medium heat and cook until heated through.
- Add the onion and pepper and stir fry for about 5-6 minutes.
- Coat the cut side of each roll with the garlic oil and sprinkle with the salt and pepper lightly.
- Place the prosciutto onto the bottom half of each roll, followed by the cheese, arugula and onion mixture.
- Cover with the top of rolls.
- Coat the outside of all sandwiches with the remaining olive oil.
- Place a grill pan over heat until heated through.
- Place the sandwiches and cook for about 2-4 minutes per side.
- Enjoy warm.

Servings Per Recipe: 4

Timing Information:

| Preparation | 10 mins |
| Total Time | 14 mins |

Nutritional Information:

Calories	276.5
Fat	25.7g
Cholesterol	19.6mg
Sodium	253.2mg
Carbohydrates	4.0g
Protein	7.9g

* Percent Daily Values are based on a 2,000 calorie diet.

PORTLAND TUNA PANINI

Ingredients

- 1 (6 oz.) cans tuna in olive oil, undrained
- 1 (6 oz.) jars artichoke hearts packed in oil, drained & chopped
- 1/8 C. sliced roasted red pepper
- 1/3 C. pitted kalamata olive, sliced
- 1 tsp minced lemon zest
- 3/4 tsp dried oregano
- 1 tbsp chopped flat-leaf parsley
- salt and pepper
- 1/2 head roasted garlic
- 1/4 C. mayonnaise
- 1 tsp Dijon mustard
- 1 tsp lemon juice
- 4 slices light rye bread
- 1 tomatoes, sliced
- 4 slices provolone cheese
- 8 slices mozzarella cheese
- olive oil

Directions

- In a bowl, add the tuna, olives, red peppers, artichokes, parsley, oregano, lemon zest, salt and pepper and mix until well combined.
- In another bowl, add the mustard, mayonnaise, roasted garlic, lemon juice and a pinch of salt and pepper and mix until well combined. Place the mayonnaise mixture onto all bread slices evenly. Place the provolone cheese onto 2 bread slice, followed by the tuna mixture, tomato slices and mozzarella.
- Cover with the remaining bread slices.
- Set your panini press as suggested by the manual.
- Coat both sides of each sandwich with the oil evenly.
- Place the sandwiches into panini press and cook until golden brown. Cut each sandwich in half and enjoy.

Servings Per Recipe: 2

Timing Information:

| Preparation | 10 mins |
| Total Time | 15 mins |

Nutritional Information:

Calories	1289.7
Fat	74.6g
Cholesterol	192.7mg
Sodium	4254.4mg
Carbohydrates	55.6g
Protein	99.7g

* Percent Daily Values are based on a 2,000 calorie diet.

WENDY'S LUNCH BOX

(HONEY CHEDDAR ON WHOLE GRAIN)

Ingredients

- 8 slices whole grain bread
- 1/4 C. honey mustard
- 2 crisp apples, sliced
- 8 oz. mild cheddar cheese, sliced
- cooking spray

Directions

- Set your panini press as suggested by the manual and lightly, grease with the cooking spray.
- Place a thin layer of the honey mustard onto all bread slices evenly.
- Place the apple slices onto 4 bread slices, followed by the cheese.
- Cover with the remaining bread slices.
- Place the sandwiches into panini press and cook for about 3-5 minutes.
- Enjoy warm.

Servings Per Recipe: 4

Timing Information:

Preparation	10 mins
Total Time	20 mins

Nutritional Information:

Calories	445.5
Fat	22.3g
Cholesterol	59.6mg
Sodium	752.9mg
Carbohydrates	40.8g
Protein	21.7g

* Percent Daily Values are based on a 2,000 calorie diet.

ARIZONA CHICKEN PANINI

Ingredients

- 2 C. cilantro, leaves and stems
- 4 garlic cloves
- 1 jalapeño, seeded and chopped
- 1/2 lime, juice of
- 2 tbsp olive oil
- 1 pinch salt
- 1/4 C. mayonnaise

- 1 tbsp canned chipotle chile puree
- 1/2 tsp sugar
- butter, softened
- 4 slices bread
- 2 oz. Monterey jack pepper cheese, sliced
- 3 oz. rotisserie cooked chicken, torn into pieces

Directions

- For the pesto: in a blender, add the jalapeño, cilantro, garlic, lime juice and salt and pulse until minced.
- While the motor is running slowly, add the oil and pulse until a paste is formed.
- In a bowl, add the chipotle puree, mayonnaise and sugar and mix until well combined.
- Place the butter onto one side of all bread slices evenly.
- Place the pesto onto other side of 2 bread slices, followed by the cheese and chicken.
- Place the mayonnaise mixture onto other side of the remaining 2 slices, followed by the chicken.
- Carefully, combine the sandwiches to make 2 sandwiches.
- Place the grill pan over medium heat until heated through.
- Place the sandwiches and cook until golden brown from both sides, pressing with the back of a spoon frequently. Enjoy warm.

Servings Per Recipe: 2

Timing Information:

Preparation	20 mins
Total Time	30 mins

Nutritional Information:

Calories	565.3
Fat	36.5g
Cholesterol	64.8mg
Sodium	735.0mg
Carbohydrates	37.5g
Protein	22.5g

* Percent Daily Values are based on a 2,000 calorie diet.

ALASKA SUMMER PANINI

Ingredients

- 8 slices brioche bread
- Dijon mustard, for spreading
- 8 thin slices gruyere cheese
- 1/2 lb. smoked salmon, sliced
- 1 lemon, grated zest
- kosher salt & ground black pepper

Directions

- Set your panini press as suggested by the manual.
- Place the mustard onto 4 bread slices, followed by the Gruyere slices, smoked salmon and lemon zest.
- Sprinkle with the salt and pepper lightly.
- Cover with the remaining bread slices.
- Place the sandwiches into panini press and cook for about 2-3 minutes.
- Cut the sandwiches in half and enjoy.

Servings Per Recipe: 4

Timing Information:

Preparation	10 mins
Total Time	13 mins

Nutritional Information:

Calories	440.5
Fat	4.8g
Cholesterol	13.0mg
Sodium	1102.2mg
Carbohydrates	73.5g
Protein	25.5g

* Percent Daily Values are based on a 2,000 calorie diet.

MEDITERRANEAN PANINI

Ingredients

- 4 boneless skinless chicken breasts
- 2 large lemons
- 2 garlic cloves, chopped
- 1 tbsp olive oil
- salt & pepper
- 2 tsp basil

- 1 loaf ciabatta
- 1/4 C. basil pesto
- 1 large tomatoes, beefsteak, sliced
- 6 oz. Italian continua, sliced
- 2 oz. bagged Baby Spinach

Directions

- Arrange the chicken breasts between 2 wax paper sheets and with a meat mallet, pound into an even thickness.
- In a bowl, add the garlic, lemon zest, lemon juice and oil and m well.
- Add the chicken and coat with the lemon mixture generously.
- Place in the fridge for about 4-20 hours.
- Place a skillet over heat until heated through.
- Add the chicken breasts and cook for about 6-8 minutes.
- Set your panini as suggested by the manual..
- Cut the ciabatta into 4 desired sized pieces.
- Place about 1 tbsp of the pesto onto both sides of the bread.
- Place the chicken onto each piece, followed by the Fontina cheese, tomatoes and spinach.
- Enjoy.

Servings Per Recipe: 4

Timing Information:

Preparation	30 mins
Total Time	45 mins

Nutritional Information:

Calories	362.2
Fat	18.6g
Cholesterol	118.1mg
Sodium	436.5mg
Carbohydrates	12.0g
Protein	40.4g

* Percent Daily Values are based on a 2,000 calorie diet.

POUND CAKE PANINI

Ingredients

- 1/4 C. chocolate hazelnut spread
- 12 slices pound cake
- 6 strawberries, hulled and sliced
- butter-flavored cooking spray

Directions

- Set your panini press as suggested by manual and grease the with the nonstick spray.
- Place the chocolate spread onto 1 side of each pound cake slices evenly.
- Place the strawberry slices onto 6 cake slices evenly.
- Cover with the remaining cake slices, chocolate side down.
- Place the sandwiches into the panini press and cook for about 2 minutes.
- Cut each sandwich in half and enjoy.

Servings Per Recipe: 6

Timing Information:

Preparation	10 mins
Total Time	12 mins

Nutritional Information:

Calories	303.3
Fat	15.6g
Cholesterol	132.6mg
Sodium	243.9mg
Carbohydrates	37.8g
Protein	4.0g

* Percent Daily Values are based on a 2,000 calorie diet.

Dijon Spinach Panini

Ingredients

- 1 tbsp butter
- 1 (8 oz.) packages mushrooms, sliced
- 4 tsp Dijon mustard
- 8 slices whole wheat bread
- 1 (5 oz.) bags spinach
- 1/4 C. roasted red pepper, sliced
- 1/4 C. chopped red onion
- 1 C. shredded gruyere cheese
- 2 tbsp butter, melted

Directions

- In a nonstick skillet, add the butter over medium-high heat and cook until melted completely.
- Add the mushrooms and stir fry for about 5-6 minutes.
- Remove from the heat.
- Place the mustard onto 4 bread slices evenly, followed by the spinach leaves, bell pepper, onion, cheese and mushrooms.
- Cover with the remaining bread slices.
- Coat both sides of all sandwiches with the melted butter.
- Place a nonstick skillet over medium-high heat until heated through.
- Add the sandwiches and top with another skillet for weight.
- Cook for about 4-6 minutes, flipping once half way through.
- Enjoy warm.

Servings Per Recipe: 4

Timing Information:

| Preparation | 10 mins |
| Total Time | 25 mins |

Nutritional Information:

Calories	356.5
Fat	19.8g
Cholesterol	52.6mg
Sodium	641.7mg
Carbohydrates	28.0g
Protein	18.6g

* Percent Daily Values are based on a 2,000 calorie diet.

PANINI VENETIAN

Ingredients

- 2 slices county-style bread
- olive oil
- 1 tbsp mayonnaise
- 2 slices mozzarella cheese
- 3 slices tomatoes
- 1 tsp balsamic vinegar
- salt & ground black pepper
- 2 basil leaves

Directions

- Set your panini press as suggested by the manual.
- Coat 1 side of both bread slices with olive oil.
- Arrange the bread slices onto a platter, oiled side down.
- Place the mayonnaise onto other side of both bread slices.
- Place the cheese onto 1 bread slice, followed by the tomato slices, vinegar, salt, pepper and basil.
- Cover with the remaining bread slice, oiled side up.
- Place the sandwich into the panini press and cook for about 3-5 minutes.
- Cut the sandwich in half and enjoy.

Servings Per Recipe: 1

Timing Information:

Preparation	5 mins
Total Time	10 mins

Nutritional Information:

Calories	379.4
Fat	19.6g
Cholesterol	49.4mg
Sodium	726.6mg
Carbohydrates	33.3g
Protein	17.3g

* Percent Daily Values are based on a 2,000 calorie diet.

PORTLAND ASIAGO PANINI

Ingredients

- 1 loaf pesto focaccia bread
- 8 oz. sliced turkey
- 4 oz. spinach artichoke spread
- 2 oz. Asiago cheese
- 1 small red onion, diced
- 1 tbsp olive oil
- 1 tbsp balsamic vinegar
- 1 -2 tomatoes, sliced
- 1 pinch salt and pepper

Directions

- Set your panini press as suggested by the manual.
- In a skillet, add the oil and cook until heated through.
- Add the onion and stir dry for about 4-5 minutes.
- Stir in the vinegar, salt and pepper and remove from the heat.
- Cut the focaccia loaf into 2 circles and then, cut each in semi-circle.
- Place the turkey onto the bottom half of the bread, followed by the spinach artichoke spread, cooked onions, Asiago cheese and tomato slices.
- Cover with the top halves of focaccia bread.
- Place the sandwich into panini press and cook for about 5 minutes.
- Enjoy hot.

Servings Per Recipe: 4

Timing Information:

Preparation	15 mins
Total Time	20 mins

Nutritional Information:

Calories	133.1
Fat	8.0g
Cholesterol	38.5mg
Sodium	39.1mg
Carbohydrates	2.8g
Protein	12.0g

* Percent Daily Values are based on a 2,000 calorie diet.

3-INGREDIENT TOMATO PANINI

Ingredients

- 8 slices whole-grain bread
- 8 slices cheddar cheese
- 1 medium tomatoes, sliced

Directions

- Arrange cheese slices over all bread slices.
- Place tomato slices onto 4 bread slices over the cheese.
- Cover with remaining bread slices.
- Grease a grill pan and place over medium-high heat until heated through.
- Place the sandwiches in batches and cook for about 3-4 minutes, flipping once half way through and pressing with the back of a spoon occasionally.
- Enjoy warm.

Servings Per Recipe: 8

Timing Information:

Preparation	5 mins
Total Time	15 mins

Nutritional Information:

Calories	182.1
Fat	10.1g
Cholesterol	29.4mg
Sodium	302.4mg
Carbohydrates	13.6g
Protein	9.0g

* Percent Daily Values are based on a 2,000 calorie diet.

FULL BREAKFAST PANINI

Ingredients

- 2 slices white bread
- 1 -2 egg
- cheddar cheese, grated
- 1 tsp butter, melted
- 2 -4 slices cooked turkey breast, sliced

Directions

- Heat a nonstick skillet and cook the egg until scrambled.
- Coat all the bread slices with butter.
- Place the cheese onto one side of bread slice, followed by the turkey and eggs.
- Cover with the remaining bread sliced.
- Place the sandwich into the panini press and cook until golden brown.
- Enjoy warm.

Servings Per Recipe: 1

Timing Information:

Preparation	5 mins
Total Time	10 mins

Nutritional Information:

Calories	238.1
Fat	10.2g
Cholesterol	196.0mg
Sodium	359.9mg
Carbohydrates	25.6g
Protein	10.1g

* Percent Daily Values are based on a 2,000 calorie diet.

4-INGREDIENT FRIENDSHIP PANINI

Ingredients

- 1 -2 slice American cheese
- 1 -2 tsp honey
- butter, melted
- 2 slices French bread

Directions

- Set your panini press as suggested by the manual.
- Coat 1 sides of all the bread slices with the melted butter evenly.
- Place a thin layer of the honey onto the other side of 1 bread, followed by the American cheese.
- Cover with the remaining bread slice, buttered side up.
- Place the sandwich into panini press and cook for about 3 minutes.
- Enjoy hot.

Servings Per Recipe: 1

Timing Information:

Preparation	5 mins
Total Time	10 mins

Nutritional Information:

Calories	
Fat	390.9
Cholesterol	2.3g
Sodium	0.0mg
Carbohydrates	656.9mg
Protein	77.9g

* Percent Daily Values are based on a 2,000 calorie diet.

AFTER SCHOOL PANINI

Ingredients

- 8 slices hearty multi grain bread
- 1/3 C. mayonnaise
- 1 C. lightly packed basil
- 1 1/2 C. sliced cooked deli-roasted chicken
- 1/2 C. bottled roasted sweet red pepper, drained and cut into strips
- 2 tbsp olive oil

Directions

- Set your sandwich press as suggested by the manual.
- Place the mayonnaise onto 1 side of all bread slices evenly.
- Place basil over 4 bread slices evenly, followed by the chicken and roasted sweet peppers.
- Cover with the remaining bread slices, mayonnaise sides down.
- Coat the out sides of all sandwiches with the oil.
- Place the sandwiches into the sandwich press and cook for about 6 minutes.
- Enjoy warm.

Servings Per Recipe: 4

Timing Information:

Preparation	10 mins
Total Time	15 mins

Nutritional Information:

Calories	144.2
Fat	13.4g
Cholesterol	5.0mg
Sodium	140.4mg
Carbohydrates	6.0g
Protein	0.7g

* Percent Daily Values are based on a 2,000 calorie diet.

KIARA'S BASIL PANINI

Ingredients

- 1/2 C. olive oil
- 3 tbsp balsamic vinegar
- 1 large garlic clove, minced
- 8 oz. sliced prosciutto, or turkey bacon
- 10 oz. sliced whole-milk mozzarella cheese
- 12 tomatoes, slices
- 12 large basil leaves
- 16 oz. ciabatta, halved horizontally
- salt
- pepper

Directions

- Set your barbecue grill to medium heat and grease the grill grate.
- In a bowl, add the garlic, vinegar, oil, salt and pepper and beat until well combined.
- Place the prosciutto onto the bottom half of bread, followed by the mozzarella, tomatoes and basil.
- Top with a slight layer of the dressing and sprinkle with the salt and pepper.
- Cover with the top half of the bread.
- With a heavy pan, press the top of the bread.
- Cut the bread into 4 equal sized portions.
- Cook the sandwiches onto the grill for about 10 minutes, flipping once half way through.
- Enjoy hot.

Servings Per Recipe: 4

Timing Information:

Preparation	15 mins
Total Time	25 mins

Nutritional Information:

Calories	530.3
Fat	43.6g
Cholesterol	56.0mg
Sodium	467.1mg
Carbohydrates	18.2g
Protein	19.1g

* Percent Daily Values are based on a 2,000 calorie diet.

NEW ENGLAND SHRIMP PANINI

Ingredients

- 1 lb. shrimp, peeled
- 4 garlic cloves, minced
- 2 tbsp lemon juice
- 1 tbsp parsley
- 1 tsp hot sauce
- 1 baguette
- 3 tbsp butter

Directions

- Set your panini press as suggested by the manual.
- Carefully, scoop most of the bread from the center of baguette.
- In a cast iron skillet, add the butter and cook until melted.
- Add the parsley, garlic, hot sauce and lemon juice and stir to combine.
- Add the shrimp and cook for about 5 minutes.
- Remove from the heat.
- Place the shrimp with pan sauce into the baguette shell
- Place the baguette into panini and cook until desired doneness.
- Enjoy warm.

Servings Per Recipe: 2

Timing Information:

Preparation	10 mins
Total Time	15 mins

Nutritional Information:

Calories	1011.8
Fat	26.5g
Cholesterol	487.5mg
Sodium	2013.5mg
Carbohydrates	121.1g
Protein	68.0g

* Percent Daily Values are based on a 2,000 calorie diet.

NOVEMBER LUNCH PANINI

Ingredients

- 4 slices Italian bread
- 2 tbsp cranberry sauce
- 2 tbsp mayonnaise
- 1 chipotle chile in adobo, chopped
- 1/2 C. spinach
- 2 slices onions
- 8 oz. sliced turkey
- 2 slices Monterey Jack cheese
- 3 tbsp olive oil

Directions

- Set your panini press as suggested by the manual.
- In a bowl, add the mayonnaise, cranberry sauce and chipotle chile and mix well.
- Place the mayonnaise mixture onto the bread slices evenly.
- Place the spinach onto 2 bread slices evenly, followed by the onion slice, turkey and cheese.
- Cover with the remaining bread slices and with your hands, flatten slightly.
- Coat the outer sides of each sandwich with the olive oil evenly.
- Place the sandwiches into panini press and cook for about 5 minutes.
- Enjoy warm.

Servings Per Recipe: 1

Timing Information:

Preparation	10 mins
Total Time	20 mins

Nutritional Information:

Calories	664.1
Fat	44.2g
Cholesterol	105.8mg
Sodium	573.8mg
Carbohydrates	32.0g
Protein	34.0g

* Percent Daily Values are based on a 2,000 calorie diet.

DORM ROOM PANINI PRESS

Ingredients

- 2 slices sliced bread
- Dijon mustard
- mayonnaise
- 3 slices brie cheese
- 2 pieces prosciutto, or salami

Directions

- Set your panini as suggested by the manual and grease it.
- Place the mayonnaise onto both bread slices, followed by the mustard.
- Place the prosciutto on 1 bread slice, followed by the cheese.
- Cover with the remaining bread slice.
- Place the sandwich into panini press and cook until golden brown.
- Enjoy warm.

Servings Per Recipe: 1

Timing Information:

Preparation	2 mins
Total Time	7 mins

Nutritional Information:

Calories	133.0
Fat	1.6g
Cholesterol	0.0mg
Sodium	255.5mg
Carbohydrates	25.3g
Protein	3.8g

* Percent Daily Values are based on a 2,000 calorie diet.

VITO'S BASIL PARMIGIANO PANINI

Ingredients

- 2 tbsp butter
- 8 slices white bread
- 1 C. shredded mozzarella cheese
- 4 whole jarred roasted red peppers, patted dry and cut into strips
- 1/4 C. grated Parmigiano-Reggiano cheese
- 12 -15 basil leaves, chopped

Directions

- In a skillet, add the butter over medium heat and cook until melted.
- Place 4 bread slices in the skillet and top each with the mozzarella, followed by the roasted red peppers and Parmigiano-Reggiano cheese.
- Cover with the remain bread slices and cook for about 1-2 minutes per side, pressing with the back of a spoon.
- Cut each sandwich into quarters and enjoy with a garnishing of the basil.

Servings Per Recipe: 4

Timing Information:

Preparation	10 mins
Total Time	15 mins

Nutritional Information:

Calories	290.6
Fat	15.0g
Cholesterol	40.9mg
Sodium	642.0mg
Carbohydrates	26.4g
Protein	12.1g

* Percent Daily Values are based on a 2,000 calorie diet.

EASY BUFFALO PANINI

Ingredients

- 6 oz. cooked chicken
- 2 tsp diced green onions
- 1/4 C. blue cheese
- 1/2 C. Baby Spinach
- 2 tsp mayonnaise
- 2 -3 tsp buffalo wing sauce
- 4 slices bread

Directions

- Set your panini press as suggested by the manual.
- In a bowl, add the wing sauce and mayonnaise and mix well.
- Place the mayonnaise mixture onto all bread slices evenly.
- Place the chicken onto 2 bread slices, followed by the onion, spinach and cheese.
- Place the sandwiches into the panini press and cook until cheese melts completely.
- Enjoy warm.

Servings Per Recipe: 2

Timing Information:

Preparation	5 mins
Total Time	10 mins

Nutritional Information:

Calories	356.0
Fat	13.8g
Cholesterol	77.7mg
Sodium	680.7mg
Carbohydrates	27.2g
Protein	29.0g

* Percent Daily Values are based on a 2,000 calorie diet.

PESTO GRILLED CHEESE PRESS

Ingredients

- 4 panini bread, sliced in half
- 6 1/2 oz. mozzarella cheese, sliced
- 1/4 C. Parmesan cheese, grated
- 1/4 C. pesto sauce
- 2 grilled bell peppers, sliced

Directions

- Place the pesto onto all bread halves evenly.
- Place the mozzarella cheese onto 4 bottom halves of bread, followed by the Parmesan cheese and peppers.
- Cover with the top halves of bread.
- Place a skillet over medium-low heat until heated through.
- Place the sandwiches and op with another heavy skillet for weight.
- Cook for about 10 minutes, flipping once half way through.
- Enjoy hot.

Servings Per Recipe: 4

Timing Information:

Preparation	15 mins
Total Time	25 mins

Nutritional Information:

Calories	177.2
Fat	12.2g
Cholesterol	41.9mg
Sodium	386.7mg
Carbohydrates	4.0g
Protein	13.1g

* Percent Daily Values are based on a 2,000 calorie diet.

ALL-AMERICAN APRICOT TURKEY PANINI

Ingredients

- 2 slices sourdough bread
- 1 -2 tbsp apricot jam
- 4 oz. sliced turkey breast
- 1 slice sweet onion
- 1/2 tbsp chopped roasted red pepper
- 2 slices Swiss cheese
- nonstick cooking spray

Directions

- Place the jam onto 1 bread slice evenly.
- Place the turkey onto the other bread slice, followed by the onion slices, roasted red peppers and Swiss cheese.
- Cover with the remaining bread slice, jam side up.
- Grease a skillet with the nonstick spray and place over medium-high until heated through.
- Place the sandwich and top with another heavy skillet for weight.
- Cook for about 1 minute per side.
- Enjoy hot.

Servings Per Recipe: 1

Timing Information:

Preparation	5 mins
Total Time	8 mins

Nutritional Information:

Calories	794.5
Fat	27.4g
Cholesterol	125.2mg
Sodium	1020.9mg
Carbohydrates	83.4g
Protein	51.4g

* Percent Daily Values are based on a 2,000 calorie diet.

Natural Peanut Butter Panini

Ingredients

- 2 slices whole wheat bread
- 1 1/2-2 tbsp natural-style peanut butter
- 1 medium banana, peeled and sliced
- 1/2 tbsp raisins
- 1/2 tbsp dried cranberries
- 1 dash cinnamon
- margarine

Directions

- Place the peanut butter onto 1 bread slice evenly, followed by the cinnamon, banana slices, raisins and cranberries.
- Cover with the remaining bread slice.
- Place a nonstick pan over medium heat until heated through.
- Cook until golden brown from both sides.
- Enjoy hot.

Servings Per Recipe: 1

Timing Information:

Preparation	6 mins
Total Time	10 mins

Nutritional Information:

Calories	400.6
Fat	14.3g
Cholesterol	0.0mg
Sodium	270.1mg
Carbohydrates	59.0g
Protein	14.7g

* Percent Daily Values are based on a 2,000 calorie diet.

Weekend Lunch Panini
(French Dip)

Ingredients

- 4 tbsp butter, softened
- 1 shallot, chopped
- 1 tbsp cornstarch
- 2 C. beef broth
- 1 lb. sliced roast beef
- 1 baguette, split lengthwise and sliced crosswise
- 4 oz. sliced Monterey Jack pepper cheese

Directions

- In a pan, add 2 tbsp of the butter over medium heat and cook until melted completely.
- Add the shallot and stir fry for about 2 minutes.
- Stir in the cornstarch and cook for about 1 minute, mixing continuously. Slowly, add the broth, beating continuously.
- Add the beef and stir to combine.
- Set the heat to low and cook until the beef is warmed.
- With tong, transfer the beef slices onto a plate, reserving the sauce.
- Place the remaining 2 tbsp of the butter onto the cut sides of each baguette piece.
- Place the roast onto 2 baguette pieces, followed by the cheese.
- Cover with the remaining baguette pieces.
- Place a nonstick grill pan over medium heat until heated through.
- Place the sandwiches and top with a heavy skillet for weight.
- Cook for about 4 minutes, flipping once half way through.
- Enjoy alongside the reserved pan sauce.

Servings Per Recipe: 4

Timing Information:

Preparation	15 mins
Total Time	25 mins

Nutritional Information:

Calories	1173.4
Fat	34.5g
Cholesterol	144.2mg
Sodium	2076.4mg
Carbohydrates	147.4g
Protein	68.9g

* Percent Daily Values are based on a 2,000 calorie diet.

5-INGREDIENT REUBEN PANINI

Ingredients

- 8 slices rye bread
- 1 (12 oz.) cans sauerkraut, drained
- 1/2 lb. corned beef
- 4 slices Swiss cheese
- butter-flavored cooking spray

Directions

- Set your panini press as suggested by the manual.
- In a microwave-safe bowl, add the sauerkraut and microwave for about 1 minute.
- Coat 1 side of all bread slices with the cooking spray evenly.
- Place the sauerkraut onto 4 bread slices, followed by the beef and cheese.
- Cover with the remaining bread slices.
- Place the sandwiches into panini press and cook until desired doneness.

Servings Per Recipe: 4

Timing Information:

Preparation	10 mins
Total Time	15 mins

Nutritional Information:

Calories	431.6
Fat	20.7g
Cholesterol	81.3mg
Sodium	1711.0mg
Carbohydrates	36.5g
Protein	24.1g

* Percent Daily Values are based on a 2,000 calorie diet.

Maria's Full Roast Beef Panini

Ingredients

- 1/4 C. mayonnaise
- 2 tsp sun-dried tomatoes, minced
- 1 tsp garlic, minced
- 1 tsp prepared horseradish
- 1 tsp ketchup
- 1 pinch cayenne pepper
- 1/3 C. red onion, slivered
- 1/3 C. pickled sweet peppers
- 1 pinch red pepper flakes
- 4 slices sourdough bread
- butter, softened
- 1/2 C. white cheddar cheese, shredded
- 4 oz. deli roast beef, sliced

Directions

- In a bowl, add the tomatoes, garlic, ketchup, horseradish, mayonnaise and cayenne and mix until well combined.
- In a separate bowl, add the peppers with some juice, onion and red pepper flakes and toss to coat well.
- Keep aside for about 6-8 minutes.
- Place the butter onto one side of all bread slices evenly.
- Place the mayonnaise mixture onto the other side of all bread slices evenly.
- Place the cheese onto 2 bread slices, followed by the beef, pepper mixture.
- Cover with the remaining bread slices, buttered side up.
- Place a skillet over medium heat until heated through.
- Add the sandwiches and top with another skillet for weight.
- Cook until golden brown from both sides.
- Enjoy warm.

Servings Per Recipe: 2

Timing Information:

Preparation	10 mins
Total Time	20 mins

Nutritional Information:

Calories	703.9
Fat	25.1g
Cholesterol	69.5mg
Sodium	1763.6mg
Carbohydrates	85.7g
Protein	34.3g

* Percent Daily Values are based on a 2,000 calorie diet.

Vegetarian Giardiniera Panini

Ingredients

- 1/2 C. pitted green olives
- 1/2 C. pitted black olives
- 1 C. giardiniera, drained
- 4 sesame seed rolls
- 8 slices sharp provolone cheese
- 1 C. marinated artichoke hearts, sliced
- 2 roasted red peppers, drained and sliced

Directions

- Set your grill to medium-high heat and lightly, grease the grill grate.
- In a blender, add the pickled veggies mix and olives and pulse until a relish like mixture is formed.
- Place the relish onto 4 bottom halves of each roll evenly, followed by 4 cheese slices, artichokes, roasted peppers and remaining cheese slices.
- Cover each with the top of rolls.
- Place the sandwiches onto grill and place a skillet on top for weight.
- Cook until golden brown from both sides.
- Enjoy warm.

Servings Per Recipe: 4

Timing Information:

Preparation	5 mins
Total Time	10 mins

Nutritional Information:

Calories	261.2
Fat	19.3g
Cholesterol	38.6mg
Sodium	938.3mg
Carbohydrates	7.5g
Protein	16.1g

* Percent Daily Values are based on a 2,000 calorie diet.

New York Provolone Breakfast Panini

Ingredients

- 4 slices crusty Italian bread
- 3 large eggs
- 3/4 tsp dried oregano
- 1/4 tsp salt
- 1/4 tsp ground black pepper
- 1/2 C. jarred roasted red pepper, drained
- 2 oz. sharp provolone cheese, sliced
- 1 oz. Parmesan cheese, sliced
- olive oil

Directions

- In a bowl, add the oregano, eggs, salt and pepper and beat well.
- Place a nonstick skillet over medium-high heat until heated through.
- Add the egg mixture and cook for about 3 minutes, lifting the edges occasionally.
- Place the cooked eggs onto 2 bread slices evenly, followed by the peppers and cheeses.
- Cover with the remaining bread slices.
- Coat the both outsides of sandwiches with the oil in a thin layer.
- Place a skillet over heat until heated through.
- Add the sandwiches and top with another skillet for weight.
- Cook, covered for about 4-6 minutes, flipping once half way through.
- Enjoy warm.

Servings Per Recipe: 2

Timing Information:

Preparation	5 mins
Total Time	15 mins

Nutritional Information:

Calories	387.3
Fat	20.6g
Cholesterol	349.2mg
Sodium	1573.6mg
Carbohydrates	23.5g
Protein	26.0g

* Percent Daily Values are based on a 2,000 calorie diet.

PANINI PARMIGIANA

Ingredients

- 16 frozen cooked Italian style meatballs
- 1 (15 oz.) cans pizza sauce
- 4 hoagie rolls
- 4 slices provolone cheese
- 1 C. loosely packed large basil leaves

Directions

- Set the broiler of your oven and arrange oven rack about 4-inch from the heating element.
- In a pan, add the pizza sauce and meatballs over medium-low heat and cook, covered for about 9-10 minutes, mixing often.
- Meanwhile, with a sharp knife, cut a thin slice from the top of all rolls, reserving the top slices.
- Carefully, scoop the center of each bread half, leaving about 1/4-1/2-inch shell.
- In the bottom of a baking sheet, arrange the rolls and roll tops, cut sides up.
- Cook under the broiler for about 1-2 minutes.
- remove from the oven and transfer the roll top slices onto a plate.
- Fill the bread rolls with the meatballs mixture, followed by the cheese.
- Cook under the broiler for about 1 minute.
- Arrange the basil leaves on top of each roll and cover each with the roll tops.
- Enjoy.

Servings Per Recipe: 4

Timing Information:

Preparation	10 mins
Total Time	23 mins

Nutritional Information:

Calories	327.6
Fat	11.2g
Cholesterol	22.5mg
Sodium	752.9mg
Carbohydrates	40.4g
Protein	15.8g

* Percent Daily Values are based on a 2,000 calorie diet.

EASY PANINI GYROS

Ingredients

- 1 skinless chicken breast half, cooked and sliced
- 1/2-1 tomatoes, sliced
- 1/4 C. feta cheese
- kalamata olive, sliced
- 1/2 tsp olive oil
- 2 slices naan bread
- tzatziki

Directions

- Set your panini press as suggested by the manual.
- Coat one side of both naan breads with olive oil evenly.
- Place the chicken onto another side of one naan bread, followed by the tomatoes, feta and olives.
- Cover with remaining naan bread, oiled side upward.
- Place the sandwich into the panini press and cook until crispy.
- Cut into 6-8 slices and enjoy alongside the tzatziki sauce.

Servings Per Recipe: 2

Timing Information:

Preparation	4 mins
Total Time	8 mins

Nutritional Information:

Calories	129.8
Fat	5.9g
Cholesterol	50.9mg
Sodium	249.1mg
Carbohydrates	1.9g
Protein	16.5g

* Percent Daily Values are based on a 2,000 calorie diet.

Amish Mushroom Panini

Ingredients

- 4 slices sandwich bread
- 1 C. shredded Fontina cheese
- 1 C. sliced mushrooms
- 1 tbsp chopped sage leaf
- salt and pepper
- 3 tbsp butter

Directions

- In a skillet, add the butter and cook until melted completely.
- Add the mushrooms and cook for about 6-7 minutes.
- Add the sage, pepper and salt and cook for about 2-3 minutes.
- Remove from the heat and keep aside.
- Set your panini press as suggested by the manual.
- Place the butter onto one side of each bread slice evenly.
- Place 2 slices into panini press, buttered side down and top with half of the cheese, followed by the mushrooms and remaining cheese.
- Cover with the remaining bread slices, buttered side up.
- Cook for about 3-4 minutes.
- Enjoy warm.

Servings Per Recipe: 2

Timing Information:

Preparation	10 mins
Total Time	15 mins

Nutritional Information:

Calories	503.4
Fat	35.8g
Cholesterol	108.4mg
Sodium	841.3mg
Carbohydrates	27.3g
Protein	18.9g

* Percent Daily Values are based on a 2,000 calorie diet.

Artisanal Handmade Focaccia for Panini's

Ingredients

- 2 1/2 tsp active dry yeast
- 2 C. warm water
- 5 C. all-purpose flour
- 1 tsp salt
- 1 tbsp olive oil
- 4 cloves garlic, peeled and chopped
- 1 tsp dried oregano
- 1/2 tsp dried rosemary
- 1/8 tsp dried marjoram
- 2 tsp chopped Italian parsley
- 1/2 tsp salt
- 1/4 tsp black pepper
- 1/4 tsp lemon pepper

Directions

- In a bread machine pan, add all the ingredients in order as suggested by the manual.
- Select the Dough cycle and press the Start button.
- After the completion of cycle, place the dough onto a lightly floured surface.
- With your hands, punch the dough and then, knead until a slightly sticky dough forms.
- Now, place the dough into a greased bowl and turn to coat completely.
- With a plastic wrap, cover the bowl and keep aside in warm place for about 1 hour.
- Set your oven to 400 degrees F and lightly grease 2 baking sheets.
- With your hands, punch the dough and then cut into 2 portions.
- With your hands, pat each dough portion into an 8x11-inch rectangle.

- In a bowl, add the garlic, parsley, rosemary, oregano and both peppers and mix well.
- Arrange 1 dough rectangle into each prepared baking sheet and coat with the oil.
- Now, place herb mixture over each rectangle evenly and with your fingers, press slightly.
- Finally, sprinkle with the salt and cook in the oven for about 20-30 minutes.
- Enjoy with your desired panini filling.

Servings Per Recipe: 1

Timing Information:

Preparation	20 mins
Total Time	40 mins

Nutritional Information:

Calories	1225.3
Fat	10.3g
Cholesterol	0.0mg
Sodium	1761.5mg
Carbohydrates	243.2g
Protein	34.7g

* Percent Daily Values are based on a 2,000 calorie diet.

French Guyana Panini

Ingredients

- 1/4 C. walnuts
- 8 1/2 inch slices French country bread
- 4 tsp apricot jam
- 6 oz. Gruyere cheese, sliced

Directions

- Set your oven to 350 degrees F before doing anything else.
- In the bottom of a baking sheet, arrange the walnuts.
- Cook in the oven for about 8-10 minutes.
- Remove from the oven and keep aside to cool.
- Then, chop the walnuts finely.
- Set your panini press as suggested by the manual.
- Place the jam onto 4 bread slices evenly, followed by the walnuts and Gruyere cheese.
- Cover with the remaining bread slices.
- Place the sandwiches into panini press and cook for about 2-4 minutes.
- Cut each sandwich into 4 slices and enjoy.

Servings Per Recipe: 1

Timing Information:

Preparation	10 mins
Total Time	24 mins

Nutritional Information:

Calories	632.8
Fat	21.0g
Cholesterol	46.8mg
Sodium	843.6mg
Carbohydrates	82.1g
Protein	29.8g

* Percent Daily Values are based on a 2,000 calorie diet.

Italian Meets Mesa Panini

Ingredients

- 8 slices sourdough bread
- 1 tbsp Worcestershire sauce
- 1 tbsp yellow mustard
- 1/3 C. mayonnaise
- 1 tbsp balsamic vinegar
- 1/4 C. red onion, chopped
- 1/4 C. cilantro, chopped
- 1/4 C. canned tomato

- 2 tbsp olive oil
- 2 tbsp butter, melted
- 1/2 tbsp garlic powder
- 1 eggplant, peeled and sliced
- 4 slices mozzarella cheese
- salt and pepper
- marinara sauce, and picante sauce

Directions

- Set your panini press as suggested by the manual.
- In a bowl, add the oil and butter and cmix well.
- Coat the eggplant slices with the oil mixture and then, sprinkle with the salt and pepper lightly.
- Heat a grill pan and cook the eggplant slices for about 2-3 minutes per side.
- Remove from the grill and place onto a plate.
- In a bowl, add the mayonnaise, mustard, vinegar, Worcestershire sauce and garlic powder and mix until well combined.
- Place the mayonnaise mixture onto 4 bread slices evenly and top with the eggplant, red onions, tomatoes, cilantro and mozzarella slice. Cover with the remaining bread slices.
- Coat the outsides of the sandwiches with the oil mixture evenly.
- Place the sandwiches into the panini press and
- cook until crisp. Enjoy warm.

Servings Per Recipe: 16

Timing Information:

Preparation	10 mins
Total Time	20 mins

Nutritional Information:

Calories	166.4
Fat	7.4g
Cholesterol	10.8mg
Sodium	304.7mg
Carbohydrates	20.4g
Protein	4.8g

* Percent Daily Values are based on a 2,000 calorie diet.

Twin City Italian Panini

Ingredients

- 8 oz. Brie round, trimmed and sliced
- 8 slices Italian bread
- 8 oz. sliced smoked turkey
- 8 fresh basil leaves
- 1/2 C. sliced strawberries
- 4 tbsp red pepper jelly
- 2 tbsp butter, melted
- 8 strawberries, halved

Directions

- Set your panini press as suggested by the manual.
- Place the jelly on one side of the 4 bread slices evenly.
- Place the turkey onto other 4 bread slices evenly, followed by the basil leaves, strawberries and Brie.
- Cover with the remaining bread slices, jelly sides down.
- Coat the outsides of sandwiches with the melted butter evenly.
- Place the sandwiches into the panini press and cook for about 2-3 minutes.
- Enjoy with a garnishing of the strawberry halves.

Servings Per Recipe: 4

Timing Information:

Preparation	15 mins
Total Time	18 mins

Nutritional Information:

Calories	467.2
Fat	24.2g
Cholesterol	95.7mg
Sodium	1158.7mg
Carbohydrates	37.7g
Protein	25.5g

* Percent Daily Values are based on a 2,000 calorie diet.

BLACKENED TUNA PANINI

Ingredients

- 7 oz. tuna, drained
- 1/3 C. green chili, chopped
- 2 tbsp onions, chopped
- 1/3 C. sour cream
- 1/2 C. Swiss cheese, grated
- 8 slices bread
- butter

Directions

- In a bowl, add the tuna, green chili, onion, sour cream and Swiss cheese and ix well.
- Place the tuna mixture onto 4 bread slices evenly.
- Cover with remaining bread slices.
- Heat a grill pan and cook the sandwiches until golden brown from both sides, pressing with the back of a spatula.
- Enjoy warm.

Servings Per Recipe: 4

Timing Information:

Preparation	5 mins
Total Time	10 mins

Nutritional Information:

Calories	303.7
Fat	11.8g
Cholesterol	39.6mg
Sodium	396.9mg
Carbohydrates	28.5g
Protein	19.9g

* Percent Daily Values are based on a 2,000 calorie diet.

TOASTED TURKEY PANINI

Ingredients

- 2 slices bread, lightly toasted
- 1/3 C. boursin cheese
- 1 medium plum tomato, sliced
- 3 oz. cooked turkey, sliced
- 2 tbsp black olive tapenade, see appendix
- drizzle extra virgin olive oil

Directions

- Set your panini press as suggested by the manual.
- Place the boursin cheese onto 1 bread slice evenly.
- Place the tapenade onto another bread slice evenly, followed by the tomato and turkey.
- Cover with the remaining bread slice.
- Coat the outsides of the sandwich with the oil evenly.
- Grill in skillet or panini press.
- Place the sandwich into the panini press and cook until golden brown.
- Enjoy warm.

Servings Per Recipe: 1

Timing Information:

Preparation	3 mins
Total Time	6 mins

Nutritional Information:

Calories	376.2
Fat	16.7g
Cholesterol	79.9mg
Sodium	394.6mg
Carbohydrates	27.7g
Protein	27.1g

* Percent Daily Values are based on a 2,000 calorie diet.

PANINI PHILADELPHIA

Ingredients

- 6 oz. shaved rib eye steaks
- 2 slices French bread, oval slices
- 2 oz. provolone cheese
- 1/2 C. sliced mushrooms
- 2 -3 tbsp butter
- salt
- pepper
- banana peppers

Directions

- In a skillet, add half the of the butter and cook until melted.
- Add the mushrooms and cook for about 4-5 minutes.
- Add the steak slices and cook until done completely.
- Stir in the salt and pepper and remove from the heat.
- Arrange the cheese onto 1 bread slice, followed by the steak mixture and banana peppers.
- Place the sandwich into the panini press and cook until golden brown.
- Enjoy warm.

Servings Per Recipe: 1

Timing Information:

Preparation	10 mins
Total Time	20 mins

Nutritional Information:

Calories	1312.6
Fat	87.9g
Cholesterol	220.9mg
Sodium	1557.8mg
Carbohydrates	75.7g
Protein	54.8g

* Percent Daily Values are based on a 2,000 calorie diet.

LEFTOVER TURKEY PANINI

Ingredients

- 2 slices sourdough bread
- 1/2 tbsp butter, softened
- 2 oz. cooked turkey
- 1/4-1/2 C. prepared stuffing
- 2 slices cheddar cheese
- ground black pepper

Directions

- Set your panini press to medium-high as suggested by the manual.
- In a microwave-safe bowl, add the stuffing and turkey and microwave until warmed through.
- Place the butter onto 1 side of all bread slices evenly.
- Arrange 1 bread slice onto a platter, buttered side down and top with 1 cheese slice, turkey mixture, black pepper and 1 cheese slice.
- Cover with the remaining bread, slice, buttered side up.
- Place the sandwich into the panini press and cook until golden brown.
- Enjoy warm.

Servings Per Recipe: 1

Timing Information:

Preparation	3 mins
Total Time	7 mins

Nutritional Information:

Calories	812.7
Fat	35.2g
Cholesterol	117.1mg
Sodium	1479.3mg
Carbohydrates	78.0g
Protein	43.4g

* Percent Daily Values are based on a 2,000 calorie diet.

Turkey Club Panini

Ingredients

- 2 slices large round bread
- 1 tbsp honey Dijon mustard
- olive oil flavored cooking spray
- butter-flavored cooking spray
- 4 slices Healthy Choice honey-roasted ham, optional
- 4 slices Healthy Choice cooked turkey
- 2 slices American cheese

Directions

- Place the mustard onto 1 bread slice evenly.
- Coat the other bread slice with the cooking spray evenly, followed by the turkey, ham and cheese slices.
- Cover with the remaining bread slice, mustard side down.
- Coat the outsides of sandwich with the cooking spray evenly.
- Place a grill pan over heat until heated through.
- Place the sandwich and top with another heavy skillet for weight and press slightly.
- Cook until cheese is melted, flipping once half way through.
- Enjoy warm.

Servings Per Recipe: 1

Timing Information:

Preparation	5 mins
Total Time	11 mins

Nutritional Information:

Calories	133.0
Fat	1.6g
Cholesterol	0.0mg
Sodium	255.5mg
Carbohydrates	25.3g
Protein	3.8g

* Percent Daily Values are based on a 2,000 calorie diet.

FRENCH GRILLED PESTO PANINI

Ingredients

- 2 French rolls, sliced in half
- 2 tbsp basil pesto
- 6 oz. grilled chicken, sliced
- 2 oz. gruyere cheese, sliced
- 1 C. arugula leaf

Directions

- Set your panini press as suggested by the manual.
- Carefully, scoop out some bread from the top and bottom halves of each bun.
- Coat outsides of buns with a thin layer of the oil.
- Place the pesto onto cut sides of each buns.
- Place the chicken onto bottom half of each bun, followed by the cheese and arugula.
- Cover with the top halves of the buns.
- Place the sandwiches into the panini press and cook until cheese melts completely.
- Place the sandwich into the panini press and cook for about 2-3 minutes.
- Enjoy warm.

Servings Per Recipe: 2

Timing Information:

Preparation	5 mins
Total Time	10 mins

Nutritional Information:

Calories	376.4
Fat	14.0g
Cholesterol	103.4mg
Sodium	393.8mg
Carbohydrates	22.2g
Protein	39.0g

* Percent Daily Values are based on a 2,000 calorie diet.

3-Ingredient Dessert Panini

Ingredients

- 2 plain croissants, halved horizontally
- 2 oz. semi-sweet chocolate chips
- 1 small banana, sliced diagonally

Directions

- Set your panini press as suggested by the manual.
- Arrange the bottom half of each croissant onto a platter, cut side up, followed by 2/3 of the chocolate, banana slices and remaining chocolate.
- Cover with the top half of each croissant, cut side down.
- Place the sandwiches into the panini press.
- Cook for about 5-7 minutes.
- Enjoy warm.

Servings Per Recipe: 2

Timing Information:

Preparation	1 min
Total Time	6 mins

Nutritional Information:

Calories	412.1
Fat	20.6g
Cholesterol	38.1mg
Sodium	427.7mg
Carbohydrates	55.5g
Protein	6.4g

* Percent Daily Values are based on a 2,000 calorie diet.

PB&J PANINI

Ingredients

- 2 slices bread
- real peanut butter
- grape jelly

Directions

- Set your panini press as suggested by the manual.
- Place the peanut butter onto 1 bread slice generously.
- Place the jelly onto another bread slice evenly.
- Arrange the both bread slices together to make a sandwich.
- Place the sandwich into the panini press and cook for about 3 minutes.
- Cut the sandwich in half and enjoy.

Servings Per Recipe: 1

Timing Information:

Preparation	3 mins
Total Time	6 mins

Nutritional Information:

Calories	133.0
Fat	1.6g
Cholesterol	0.0mg
Sodium	255.5mg
Carbohydrates	25.3g
Protein	3.8g

* Percent Daily Values are based on a 2,000 calorie diet.

EUROPEAN BEEF PANINI

Ingredients

- 8 slices of rustic country bread
- 1/2 C. mayonnaise
- 1/4 C. prepared horseradish sauce
- 1/2 lb. roast beef, sliced
- 1 red pepper
- 8 slices tomatoes
- 8 slices Havarti cheese
- 2 tsp olive oil
- 1 garlic clove
- herbs

Directions

- In a bowl, add the horseradish and mayonnaise and mix well.
- Coat 1 side of each bread slice with the oil evenly and then, rub with the garlic clove.
- Arrange 4 bread slices onto a platter, oiled side down.
- Place the horseradish mixture onto each bread slice and top with the roast beef, followed by pepper rings, tomato and cheese
- Cover with the remaining bread slices.
- Place a grill pan over heat until heated through.
- Place the sandwich onto grill pan and top with weigh with a heavy skillet for weight.
- Cook until golden brown from both sides.
- Cut each sandwich in half and enjoy with a garnishing of the herbs.

Servings Per Recipe: 4

Timing Information:

Preparation	15 mins
Total Time	25 mins

Nutritional Information:

Calories	816.2
Fat	34.0g
Cholesterol	109.7mg
Sodium	1374.5mg
Carbohydrates	83.8g
Protein	44.9g

* Percent Daily Values are based on a 2,000 calorie diet.

MEXICAN SEAFOOD PANINI

Ingredients

- 4 tilapia fillets
- 1 C. Club crackers, crushed
- 1/4 tsp ground black pepper
- 1 egg, beaten
- oil
- 1 tbsp butter
- 1 small jalapeño, diced
- 1 garlic clove, minced

- 1 1/2 tbsp flour
- 1 C. chicken broth
- 1/4 C. sour cream
- 8 slices hearty country Italian bread
- 2 tbsp olive oil
- 2 Roma tomatoes, sliced
- 8 slices provolone cheese

Directions

- In a shallow bowl, place the eggs.
- In another bowl, add the crackers and pepper and mix well.
- Dip the tilapia fillets into the egg and then dredge with the cracker mixture.
- In a deep skillet, heat the oil until its temperature reaches to 350 degree F.
- Add the tilapia fillets and cook until desired doneness.
- With a slotted spoon transfer tilapia fillets onto a paper towel-lined plate to drain.
- Meanwhile, for the sauce: in a skillet, add the butter over low heat and cook until melted.
- Add the garlic and jalapeño and stir fry for about 2 minutes.
- Add the flour and cook for about 1 minute, mixing continuously.
- Add the chicken broth and cook until sauce becomes thick, mixing continuously.
- Stir in the sour cream and remove from the heat.
- Coat 1 side of all bread slices with the olive oil evenly.

- Arrange 4 bread slices onto a platter, oiled side down and top with the provolone cheese, tomato slices, tilapia fillet and cream sauce.
- Cover with the remaining bread slices, oil side up.
- Heat a greased cast iron grill pan over medium heat.
- Place the sandwiches and top with a heavy cast iron skillet for weight and press down slightly.
- Cook for about 1-2 minutes per side.
- Enjoy warm.

Servings Per Recipe: 4

Timing Information:

Preparation	20 mins
Total Time	55 mins

Nutritional Information:

Calories	649.7
Fat	35.9g
Cholesterol	162.7mg
Sodium	1144.8mg
Carbohydrates	33.9g
Protein	47.6g

* Percent Daily Values are based on a 2,000 calorie diet.

VICTORIAN TOMATO PANINI

Ingredients

- 1 baguette, halved horizontally, toasted
- 2 tbsp extra virgin olive oil
- 2 large tomatoes, sliced
- 1 lb. mozzarella cheese, sliced
- 1 pinch dried oregano
- 12 basil leaves
- 1 avocado, sliced
- salt and pepper

Directions

- Coat both halves of the bread with olive oil evenly.
- Place the tomato onto bottom half of the bread, followed by the salt, pepper, Mozzarella, dried Oregano, olive oil, basil leaves, avocado, salt and pepper.
- Cover with t top half of the bred.
- Cut the sandwich into desired sized slices and enjoy.

Servings Per Recipe: 2

Timing Information:

Preparation	5 mins
Total Time	10 mins

Nutritional Information:

Calories	1615.5
Fat	86.1g
Cholesterol	179.1mg
Sodium	2819.7mg
Carbohydrates	138.5g
Protein	73.9g

* Percent Daily Values are based on a 2,000 calorie diet.

Chicago Brie Panini

Ingredients

- 4 tbsp unsalted butter, softened
- 2 tsp unsalted butter, softened
- 1 scallion, chopped
- 1/2 tsp lemon juice
- 1/4 tsp Dijon mustard
- 4 soft hoagie rolls
- 3/4 lb. sliced prosciutto, or roast beef
- 1/2 lb. Brie cheese, rind removed, cheese cut into pieces
- 1 large granny smith apple, peeled, cored and sliced

Directions

- In a bowl, add 4 tbsp of the butter and beat until creamy.
- Add the mustard, scallion and lemon juice and beat until smooth.
- Place a griddle over low heat until heated through.
- Place the scallion butter on the cut sides of the rolls. Lay the prosciutto on the bottom halves; top with the Brie and the apple slices and close the sandwiches. Lightly spread the remaining 2 tsp of butter on the outside of the rolls (it will be a very thin layer).
- Put the sandwiches on the griddle. Cover with a heavy skillet and cook over low heat, turning occasionally, until toasted and the Brie is melted, 10 minutes. Cut the panini in half and serve.

Servings Per Recipe: 4

Timing Information:

Preparation	5 mins
Total Time	15 mins

Nutritional Information:

Calories	504.2
Fat	31.6g
Cholesterol	92.3mg
Sodium	673.1mg
Carbohydrates	37.9g
Protein	17.7g

* Percent Daily Values are based on a 2,000 calorie diet.

Sun Dried Summer Panini

Ingredients

- 1 eggplant, sliced
- 2 tsp olive oil
- 1 loaf ciabatta
- 1/3 C. mayonnaise
- 2 oz. sun-dried tomatoes packed in oil, drained and diced
- 6 oz. mozzarella cheese

Directions

- Coat the eggplant slices with the oil evenly and sprinkle with the salt and pepper slightly.
- Place a grill pan over heat until heated through.
- Add the eggplant slices and cook for about 2-3 minutes per side.
- Cut the bread into 4 pieces and then, cut each in half lengthwise.
- In a bowl, add the sun dried tomatoes and mayonnaise and mix well.
- Place the mayonnaise mixture onto 1 side of the ciabatta pieces evenly.
- Place the grilled eggplant slices onto bottom halves of ciabatta pieces, followed by the cheese.
- Cover with the top halves of ciabatta pieces.
- Coat the outsides of the sandwiches with the oil evenly.
- Cook the sandwiches onto the grill pan until golden brown from both sides.
- Enjoy hot.

Servings Per Recipe: 4

Timing Information:

Preparation	10 mins
Total Time	15 mins

Nutritional Information:

Calories	281.4
Fat	20.5g
Cholesterol	38.6mg
Sodium	445.7mg
Carbohydrates	15.4g
Protein	11.4g

* Percent Daily Values are based on a 2,000 calorie diet.

Spicy Beef Panini with Caribbean Aioli

Ingredients

- 10 slices sourdough bread
- 2 (4 oz.) cans whole green chilies
- 1 lb. deli sliced roast beef
- 5 slices sharp cheddar cheese
- 4 oz. mozzarella cheese, grated
- 4 tbsp lime juice
- 1 garlic clove, minced
- 1/2 tsp hot sauce
- 1 tsp Dijon mustard
- 1 C. cilantro leaves, chopped
- 1 C. mayonnaise
- salt and pepper

Directions

- Set your panini press to medium as suggested by the manual and grease it.
- In a bowl, add the cilantro, garlic, mayonnaise, mustard, lime juice, hot sauce, salt and pepper and mix until well combined.
- Keep aside until using.
- Place the mayonnaise mixture onto all the bread slices evenly.
- Place the cheese onto 5 bread slices, followed by the roast beef, green chili and mozzarella cheese.
- Cover with the remaining bread slices.
- Place the sandwiches into the panini press and cook until golden brown.
- Enjoy warm.

Servings Per Recipe: 5

Timing Information:

Preparation	5 mins
Total Time	10 mins

Nutritional Information:

Calories	903.3
Fat	41.6g
Cholesterol	123.9mg
Sodium	1508.2mg
Carbohydrates	84.2g
Protein	49.0g

* Percent Daily Values are based on a 2,000 calorie diet.

CINNAMON APPLE PANINI

Ingredients

- 8 slices whole wheat bread
- 1 apple, peeled, cored, then chopped
- 1/2-1 C. shredded cheddar cheese
- 1/8 C. granulated sugar
- 1/4 tsp cinnamon
- 2 tbsp butter
- cooking spray

Directions

- Set your panini press as suggested by the manual.
- In a bowl, mix add the sugar and cinnamon and mix.
- Add the apple pieces and toss to coat well.
- Grease a pan with the cooking spray lightly and heat it.
- Place 4 bread slices and top each with half of the cheese evenly, followed by the apple mixture, 1 tbsp of the butter and the remaining cheese.
- Cover with the remaining bread slices.
- Place the remaining butter onto outsides of each sandwich evenly and sprinkle with the cinnamon sugar lightly.
- Place the sandwich into the panini press and cook until golden brown.
- Enjoy warm.

Servings Per Recipe: 4

Timing Information:

Preparation	5 mins
Total Time	12 mins

Nutritional Information:

Calories	288.0
Fat	12.8g
Cholesterol	30.1mg
Sodium	424.1mg
Carbohydrates	37.1g
Protein	9.1g

* Percent Daily Values are based on a 2,000 calorie diet.

ALTERNATIVE TURKEY SALAD PANINI

Ingredients

- 2 slices whole wheat bread
- 1 tsp mayonnaise
- 2 slices cooked turkey
- 2 slices mozzarella cheese
- 1 orange, 3 segments used
- cilantro
- salt

Directions

- Set your panini press as suggested by the manual.
- Place the mayonnaise onto both bread slices evenly.
- Place the chicken onto 1 bread slice, followed by the cheese, orange segments and cilantro.
- Sprinkle with the salt and cover with the remaining bread slice.
- Place the sandwich into the panini press and cook until golden brown.
- Enjoy warm.

Servings Per Recipe: 1

Timing Information:

Preparation	10 mins
Total Time	20 mins

Nutritional Information:

Calories	391.8
Fat	17.0g
Cholesterol	46.9mg
Sodium	692.3mg
Carbohydrates	43.6g
Protein	19.5g

* Percent Daily Values are based on a 2,000 calorie diet.

Australian Sweet Panini

Ingredients

- 1 C. chocolate hazelnut spread, warmed
- 8 slices white bread, chopped
- 2 bananas, sliced lengthwise
- 16 marshmallows, halved, optional
- butter, softened
- powdered sugar

Directions

- Set your grill for medium-low heat and lightly, grease the grill grate.
- Place a thin layer of the warm hazelnut spread onto all bread slices.
- Place the banana slices onto 4 bread slices.
- Place the marshmallows onto the remaining 4 bread slices.
- Arrange the slices together to make sandwiches and press slightly.
- Place a thin layer of the butter onto outsides of each sandwich.
- Cook the sandwich onto the grill for about 4 minutes, flipping once half way through.
- Enjoy warm.

Servings Per Recipe: 1

Timing Information:

Preparation	10 mins
Total Time	14 mins

Nutritional Information:

Calories	337.4
Fat	11.9g
Cholesterol	0.0mg
Sodium	154.4mg
Carbohydrates	53.7g
Protein	4.4g

* Percent Daily Values are based on a 2,000 calorie diet.

Panini Moscow

Ingredients

- 2 (12 inch) hoagie rolls
- 1 tbsp olive oil
- 3 oz. prepared Russian salad dressing
- 4 slices provolone cheese
- 6 slices deli roast beef
- 6 slices deli corned beef
- 4 slices tomatoes

Directions

- Set your panini press to medium as suggested by the manual.
- Coat the outside of rolls with the olive oil evenly.
- Place the salad dressing onto the insides of all rolls evenly.
- Place the cheese onto bottom half of each roll, followed by the roast beef slices, corned beef slices and tomato slices.
- Cut each roll in half.
- Place the sandwiches into the panini press and cook until golden brown.
- Enjoy warm.

Servings Per Recipe: 2

Timing Information:

Preparation	5 mins
Total Time	7 mins

Nutritional Information:

Calories	646.5
Fat	49.9g
Cholesterol	130.7mg
Sodium	2034.8mg
Carbohydrates	16.4g
Protein	33.2g

* Percent Daily Values are based on a 2,000 calorie diet.

5-Ingredient English Roast Beef Panini

Ingredients

- 4 soft sourdough rolls
- 10 -12 oz. blue cheese
- 8 -10 oz. rare roast beef, sliced
- watercress leaf
- soft butter

Directions

- Place the blue cheese onto both sides of each roll generously.
- Place the roast beef onto bottom half of each roll, followed by the watercress leaves.
- Cover with the top halves and press well to seal.
- Place a thin layer of the butter onto outsides of each sandwich.
- Place a heavy-bottomed skillet over medium-high heat until heated through.
- Place the sandwiches in batches and top with another heavy skillet for weight and press firmly.
- Cook until golden brown from both sides.
- Enjoy warm.

Servings Per Recipe: 4

Timing Information:

Preparation	15 mins
Total Time	25 mins

Nutritional Information:

Calories	353.3
Fat	25.1g
Cholesterol	93.3mg
Sodium	1019.8mg
Carbohydrates	1.6g
Protein	30.3g

* Percent Daily Values are based on a 2,000 calorie diet.

NAPA VALLEY FIG PANINI

Ingredients

- 1/4 C. fig preserves
- 1 (8 oz.) ciabatta, cut lengthwise
- 1/4 C. crumbled blue cheese
- 2 tbsp butter, softened
- 8 oz. sliced cooked chicken breasts
- 1/8 tsp ground black pepper
- 2 C. arugula leaves
- 1 tsp lemon juice

Directions

- In a bowl, add the butter and cheese and stir until smooth.
- Place the jam onto cut side of top half of bread evenly.
- Spread the cheese mixture over cut side of bottom half of bread, followed by the chicken.
- Sprinkle with the pepper and cover with the top half of bread, jam side down.
- Place a nonstick skillet over medium heat until heated through.
- Place the sandwich in skillet and cover with another heavy skillet for weight.
- Cook for about 5 minutes, flipping once half way through.
- Meanwhile, in a bowl, add the arugula and lemon juice and gently, toss to coat.
- Remove the top half of bread from sandwich.
- Place the arugula mixture over chicken and cover with the top bread half.
- Cut sandwich into 4 equal sized pieces and enjoy.

Servings Per Recipe: 4

Timing Information:

Preparation	10 mins
Total Time	20 mins

Nutritional Information:

Calories	250.9
Fat	12.6g
Cholesterol	69.2mg
Sodium	208.0mg
Carbohydrates	14.4g
Protein	19.1g

* Percent Daily Values are based on a 2,000 calorie diet.

COUNTRY TARRAGON CHICKEN PANINI

Ingredients

- 3/4 C. reduced-fat mayonnaise
- 1/4 C. tarragon, chopped
- 4 tsp tarragon vinegar
- 2 boneless skinless chicken breast halves
- 3 tbsp olive oil
- 6 garlic cloves, minced
- 3 medium zucchini, trimmed, sliced lengthwise
- 1 large red onion, sliced
- 4 kaiser rolls, split horizontally
- 8 slices tomatoes

Directions

- Set your barbecue grill to medium-high heat.
- In a bowl, add the vinegar, mayonnaise, vinegar, tarragon, salt and pepper and mix well. With a meat mallet, flatten each chicken breast half into 1/2-inch thickness. Now, cut each pounded chicken breast half into half crosswise. Coat chicken pieces with 1 tbsp of the oil and season with half of the garlic, salt and pepper.
- Coat the zucchini and onion slices with the remaining 2 tbsp of the oil and season with the remaining garlic, salt and pepper.
- Cook the chicken pieces onto the grill for about 10 minutes, flipping once half way through. Remove from the grill and place the chicken pieces onto a plate. Now, cook the onion onto the grill for about 14 minutes, flipping once half way through. Cook the zucchini onto the grill for about 10 minutes, flipping once half way through.
- Remove from the grill and place the vegetables onto another plate.
- Now, cook the rolls onto the grill for about 4 minutes, flipping once half way through. Place the mayonnaise mixture onto bottom half of each roll evenly, followed by the chicken, grilled vegetables and tomato slices. Cover with the top halves and enjoy.

Servings Per Recipe: 4

Timing Information:

Preparation	10 mins
Total Time	30 mins

Nutritional Information:

Calories	539.0
Fat	28.8g
Cholesterol	49.9mg
Sodium	728.8mg
Carbohydrates	48.0g
Protein	23.3g

* Percent Daily Values are based on a 2,000 calorie diet.

BRIANNA'S FAVORITE PANINI

Ingredients

- 1 loaf ciabatta
- 4 tbsp basil pesto
- 4 slices smoked provolone cheese
- 1 bunch arugula
- 12 slices black forest ham, or honey turkey
- olive oil
- 2 roma tomatoes, sliced
- 3 tbsp mayonnaise

Directions

- Set your panini press to medium as suggested by the manual.
- Cut a thin slice from the top of the ciabatta loaf to make the top flat.
- Now, cut loaf into four equal sized pieces and then, cut each one in half.
- Coat the outside of each bread piece with a thin layer of the oil.
- Place the mayonnaise onto the inside of 4 bread pieces evenly.
- Place 1 tbsp of the pesto onto the inside of other 4 bread pieces and top with the arugula, followed by the provolone, tomato and ham.
- Cover with the remaining bread pieces.
- Place the sandwiches into the panini press and cook for about 2-4 minutes.
- Enjoy warm.

Servings Per Recipe: 4

Timing Information:

Preparation	5 mins
Total Time	10 mins

Nutritional Information:

Calories	246.5
Fat	14.8g
Cholesterol	67.2mg
Sodium	1342.1mg
Carbohydrates	6.5g
Protein	21.7g

* Percent Daily Values are based on a 2,000 calorie diet.

Honey Dijon Beef and Onions Panini

Ingredients

- 3 sweet onions, sliced
- 2 tbsp honey
- 1 tbsp Dijon mustard
- 1 tbsp apple cider vinegar
- black pepper
- softened butter
- 8 slices rye bread
- 3/4 lb. sliced deli roast beef
- 8 slices American cheese

Directions

- Set your panini press as suggested by the manual.
- In a pot, add the vinegar, onions, mustard, honey and black pepper over medium heat and cook for about 8-10 minutes, mixing frequently.
- Coat the both sides of each bread slice evenly.
- Place the roast beef onto 4 bread slices, followed by the cheese slices and onion mixture.
- Cover with the remaining bread slice.
- Place the sandwiches into the panini press and cook until golden brown.
- Enjoy warm.

Servings Per Recipe: 1

Timing Information:

Preparation	20 mins
Total Time	20 mins

Nutritional Information:

Calories	694.7
Fat	27.8g
Cholesterol	176.7mg
Sodium	3897.3mg
Carbohydrates	53.6g
Protein	55.5g

* Percent Daily Values are based on a 2,000 calorie diet.

PEARS ON FOCACCIA PANINI

Ingredients

- 1 ripe pear, peeled, cored, and cut into wedges
- 1/2 tsp sugar
- 1 loaf focaccia bread, halved horizontally
- 4 tsp balsamic vinegar
- 1 C. trimmed arugula
- 1/2 C. pecorino Romano cheese, shaved
- 4 oz. prosciutto, slices
- cracked pepper

Directions

- Place a nonstick skillet over medium-high heat until heated through.
- Add the pear wedges and sugar and cook for about 4 minutes, flipping once half way through.
- Coat the cut sides of bread loaf with the vinegar.
- Place the pear slices onto bottom half of the bread, followed by the arugula, cheese and prosciutto.
- Sprinkle with the pepper generously and cover with the top half of bread.
- Place the nonstick skillet over medium-high heat until heated through.
- Place the sandwich and top with another heavy skillet for weight.
- Cook for about 8 minutes, flipping once half way through.
- Cut the sandwich into 4 equal sized portions and enjoy.

Servings Per Recipe: 4

Timing Information:

Preparation	5 mins
Total Time	11 mins

Nutritional Information:

Calories	27.3
Fat	0.0g
Cholesterol	0.0mg
Sodium	1.7mg
Carbohydrates	7.1g
Protein	0.2g

* Percent Daily Values are based on a 2,000 calorie diet.

THE QUEEN'S RADICCHIO PANINI

Ingredients

- 4 English muffins, split and toasted
- 3 tbsp pesto sauce, prepared
- 4 oz. goat cheese
- 4 slices tomatoes, large
- 8 leaves radicchio

Directions

- Set your panini press to medium as suggested by the manual and grease it.
- Place the pesto onto toasted side of each English muffin.
- Place the cheese onto 4 muffin halves, followed by the tomato slices and radicchio.
- Top with the remaining English muffin halves.
- Place the sandwich into the panini press and cook for about 4 minutes.
- Enjoy warm.

Servings Per Recipe: 4

Timing Information:

Preparation	30 mins
Total Time	30 mins

Nutritional Information:

Calories	240.0
Fat	9.5g
Cholesterol	22.4mg
Sodium	357.1mg
Carbohydrates	27.3g
Protein	11.5g

* Percent Daily Values are based on a 2,000 calorie diet.

Dijon Tuna Panini

Ingredients

- 6 tbsp mayonnaise
- 2 (8 oz.) jars tuna, packed in olive oil, drained
- 1 tbsp lemon juice
- 1 tsp Dijon mustard
- 1/4 C. celery, diced
- 6 cloves mashed roasted garlic
- 2 tbsp flat leaf parsley, chopped
- 1 tbsp capers, drained
- 1/4 tsp celery seed
- kosher salt & ground black pepper
- 8 slices of multi grain sandwich bread
- 4 oz. Gruyere cheese, sliced

Directions

- Set your oven to 300 degrees F before doing anything else and line a baking sheet with a piece of the foil.
- Arrange the unpeeled garlic cloves onto prepared baking sheet and drizzle with the olive oil. Seal the foil around garlic cloves and cook in the oven for about 30 minutes. Remove the garlic cloves from oven and keep aside to cool. After cooling, remove the peel of garlic cloves and with a fork, mash them. Set your panini press to medium as suggested by the manual. In a bowl, add the mayonnaise, mustard, 1 tbsp of the reserved tuna oil, lemon juice, capers, garlic, celery, parsley, celery seeds, salt and pepper and mix until well combined. Add the tuna and gently, stir to combine.
- Place the tuna mixture onto 4 bread slices, followed by the Gruyere cheese. Cover with the remaining bread slices.
- Place the sandwiches into the panini press and cook until cheese melts completely. Enjoy warm.

Servings Per Recipe: 4

Timing Information:

Preparation	20 mins
Total Time	30 mins

Nutritional Information:

Calories	510.5
Fat	23.9g
Cholesterol	80.0mg
Sodium	636.8mg
Carbohydrates	32.9g
Protein	39.4g

* Percent Daily Values are based on a 2,000 calorie diet.

GREEK MUSHROOM PANINI

Ingredients

- 4 sun-dried tomatoes
- 4 portabella mushroom caps, stemmed and halved
- 1/4 C. crumbled gorgonzola cheese
- 1 tbsp olive oil
- 1 tsp olive oil
- salt and pepper

Directions

- In a bowl of the boiling water, add the sun dried tomatoes for about 10 minutes.
- Drain the tomatoes well and then, chop them.
- Place about 1 tbsp of the chopped tomatoes onto each mushroom half, followed by 1 tbsp of the cheese.
- Top with remaining mushroom slices.
- Coat the top side of each mushroom sandwich with the olive oil.
- Place a grill pan over heat until heated through.
- Place the mushroom sandwiches, oiled side down and cook for about 2 minutes.
- Flip and coat the mushroom with the oil.
- Cook for about 2 minutes.
- Sprinkle with the salt and pepper and enjoy.
- Enjoy warm.

Servings Per Recipe: 2

Timing Information:

| Preparation | 15 mins |
| Total Time | 25 mins |

Nutritional Information:

Calories	193.1
Fat	14.3g
Cholesterol	12.6mg
Sodium	329.4mg
Carbohydrates	11.1g
Protein	8.3g

* Percent Daily Values are based on a 2,000 calorie diet.

GRILLED ZUCCHINI AND EGGPLANT PANINI

Ingredients

- 3/4 C. extra virgin olive oil
- 2 large garlic cloves, crushed
- 1 eggplant, peeled lengthwise in 2 places to make stripes
- 1 zucchini, sliced lengthwise
- salt and pepper
- herbes de provence, see appendix
- 2 bell peppers, quartered lengthwise
- 1 loaf ciabatta, split horizontally
- 8 slices Swiss cheese
- 2 C. arugula leaves
- 1/3 C. olive tapenade, see appendix

Directions

- Set your grill for medium heat and lightly, grease the grill grate.
- In a pan, add the olive oil and garlic over medium heat and cook until heated completely. Remove from the heat.
- Coat the zucchini and eggplant slices with the garlic oil evenly and sprinkle with the herbes de provence, salt and pepper.
- Cook the zucchini, eggplant and bell peppers onto the grill for about 3-4 minutes per side. Place the tapenade onto the top half of bread.
- Place the vegetables onto the bottom half of bread loaf, followed by the cheese and arugula. Cover with the top half of bread.
- Place sandwich onto the grill and top with 2 foil covered bricks.
- Press the sandwich and cook for about 4 minutes, flipping once half way through. Cut into 4 equal sized pieces and enjoy.

Servings Per Recipe: 4

Timing Information:

Preparation	5 mins
Total Time	15 mins

Nutritional Information:

Calories	623.2
Fat	56.5g
Cholesterol	51.5mg
Sodium	120.3mg
Carbohydrates	14.9g
Protein	17.7g

* Percent Daily Values are based on a 2,000 calorie diet.

CHICKEN AND RANCH PANINI

Ingredients

- 8 tbsp softened unsalted butter
- 2 oz. Ranch® Dressing and Seasoning Mix
- 2 boneless skinless chicken breasts
- 1/2 C. water
- 8 slices bakery sourdough bread

- 4 oz. softened cream cheese
- 1/4 C. chopped black olives
- 1/2 C. canned artichoke heart, diced
- 4 tsp pimientos
- 1 tbsp grated lemon zest
- 1/3 C. grated Parmesan cheese
- 2 C. baby spinach leaves

Directions

- For the ranch butter: in a bowl, add 2 tbsp of the dressing seasoning mix and 6 tbsp of the butter and mix well.
- Keep aside.
- Season the chicken with 4 tsp of the dressing seasoning mix evenly.
- In a skillet. add the remaining butter over medium-high heat and cook until melted.
- Add the chicken breast and cook for about 8 minutes, flipping once half way through.
- Add the water and cook, covered until chicken is done completely.
- Remove from the heat and keep aside for about 5 minutes.
- Transfer the chicken breasts onto a cutting board and cut each into 4 thin pieces horizontally.
- Return the chicken into the skillet and toss t cat with cooking liquid.
- Meanwhile, for the cheese spread,: in a bowl, add the Parmesan cheese, cream cheese, pimentos, artichokes, olives, lemon zest and dressing seasoning mix and mix until blended nicely.

- Set your panini press as suggested by the manual.
- Place the ranch butter onto all bread slices.
- Place the cheese spread onto unbuttered side of 4 butter slices.
- Place other 4 bread slices onto a platter, buttered side down.
- Place the chicken onto bread slices, followed by the spinach leaves.
- Cover with the remaining bread slices, buttered side up.
- Place the sandwiches into the panini press and cook for about 8 minutes.
- Enjoy warm.

Servings Per Recipe: 4

Timing Information:

Preparation	5 mins
Total Time	35 mins

Nutritional Information:

Calories	799.6
Fat	40.0g
Cholesterol	137.3mg
Sodium	1034.3mg
Carbohydrates	77.7g
Protein	33.8g

* Percent Daily Values are based on a 2,000 calorie diet.

ITALIAN CHICKEN PANINI

Ingredients

- 1/2 C. Italian Dressing, divided
- 1/2 lb. boneless skinless chicken breast half
- 1 red pepper, cut into strips
- 1 small zucchini, cut lengthwise in half, sliced crosswise
- 4 slices Italian bread
- 1/2 C. Shredded Mozzarella Cheese
- 2 tbsp chopped basil

Directions

- In a bowl, reserve 1 tbsp of the dressing.
- In a bowl, add the chicken, vegetables and remaining dressing and mix well.
- Place in the fridge for about 35-40 minutes.
- Remove the chicken and vegetables from the bowl, discarding the marinade.
- Place a skillet over medium heat until heated through.
- Add the chicken and vegetables and cook for about 9-10 minutes, flipping once half way through.
- Set your panini press as suggested by the manual.
- Place the chicken mixture onto 2 bread slices, followed by the cheese and basil.
- Cover with the remaining bread slices.
- Coat the outsides of the sandwiches with the reserved dressing.
- Place the sandwich into the panini press and cook for about 5 minutes.
- Enjoy warm.

Servings Per Recipe: 2

Timing Information:

Preparation	10 mins
Total Time	10 mins

Nutritional Information:

Calories	266.8
Fat	4.7g
Cholesterol	72.6mg
Sodium	372.4mg
Carbohydrates	25.4g
Protein	29.0g

* Percent Daily Values are based on a 2,000 calorie diet.

Pesto Caprese Panini

Ingredients

- 1/2 loaf Italian bread, halved vertically
- 1/4 C. pesto sauce
- 8 -12 oz. Brie cheese, rind removed
- 1 large tomatoes, sliced
- extra virgin olive oil
- kosher salt and cracked black pepper

Directions

- Set your panini press as suggested by the manual.
- Coat insides of the bread halves with the olive oil generously.
- Now, coat the outside of the bread halves with a thin layer of the olive oil.
- Season the tomato slices with the salt and pepper.
- Place the pesto onto the bottom half of bread, followed by the tomato slices and Brie chunks.
- Cover with the top half of bread.
- Place the sandwich into the panini press and cook until golden brown.
- Cut the sandwich into desired sized pieces and enjoy.

Servings Per Recipe: 4

Timing Information:

Preparation	10 mins
Total Time	25 mins

Nutritional Information:

Calories	299.1
Fat	17.1g
Cholesterol	56.7mg
Sodium	577.9mg
Carbohydrates	20.7g
Protein	15.4g

* Percent Daily Values are based on a 2,000 calorie diet.

Dijon Mushroom and Zucchini Panini

Ingredients

- 3 -4 slices Havarti with dill
- 2 slices square sourdough bread
- 2 slices white mushrooms
- 2 slices onions
- 3 slices tomatoes, remove the seeds
- 3 slices zucchini
- 1 -2 leaf red leaf lettuce, washed and dried
- 5 -6 sliced black olives

Spread

- 1 -2 tsp horseradish
- 1 tbsp Dijon mustard
- 1/4 C. egg less mayonnaise
- 1 tbsp olive oil, place in a mug

Directions

- Set your panini press as suggested by the manual.
- For the sauce: in a bowl, add all the ingredients and mix until well combined.
- Place some of the sauce onto both bread slices evenly.
- Place the lettuce onto 1 bread slice, followed by the tomato, onion, mushrooms, zucchini, olives and Havarti.
- Cover with the remaining bread slice.
- Coat the outside of sandwich with oil evenly.
- Place the sandwich into the panini press and cook until golden brown.
- Enjoy warm.

Servings Per Recipe: 1

Timing Information:

| Preparation | 10 mins |
| Total Time | 12 mins |

Nutritional Information:

Calories	769.4
Fat	40.0g
Cholesterol	15.2mg
Sodium	1584.7mg
Carbohydrates	90.5g
Protein	14.3g

* Percent Daily Values are based on a 2,000 calorie diet.

PROVOLONE PROSCIUTTO PANINI

Ingredients

- 2 slices bread
- 3 slices prosciutto, or turkey
- 1 jarred roasted red pepper
- 2 slices provolone cheese
- olive oil

Directions

- Place the prosciutto onto 1 bread slice, followed by the pepper and cheese.
- Cover with the remaining bread slice.
- Place a lightly greased grill pan over heat until heated through.
- Place the sandwich and top with a heavy skillet for weight.
- Cook until golden brown from both sides.
- Enjoy warm.

Servings Per Recipe: 1

Timing Information:

Preparation	1 mins
Total Time	5 mins

Nutritional Information:

Calories	462.5
Fat	18.2g
Cholesterol	38.6mg
Sodium	1171.5mg
Carbohydrates	51.8g
Protein	21.9g

* Percent Daily Values are based on a 2,000 calorie diet.

CORNED BEEF ON PUMPERNICKEL PANINI

Ingredients

- 4 slices pumpernickel bread
- 1 tbsp butter, melted
- 2 tbsp spicy mustard
- 4 oz. corned beef, sliced
- 2 oz. Fontina cheese, sliced
- 6 slices dill pickles
- 4 thin slices onions

Directions

- Set your panini press to high as suggested by the manual.
- Coat one side of all the bread slices with the butter evenly.
- Place the bread slices onto a platter, buttered side down.
- Place the mustard onto another side of all slices.
- Place the beef onto 2 bread slices, followed by the cheese, pickle and onion.
- Cover with the remaining bread slices and gently, press each one.
- Place the sandwich into the panini press and cook for about 3-4 minutes.
- Enjoy hot.

Servings Per Recipe: 2

Timing Information:

Preparation	15 mins
Total Time	19 mins

Nutritional Information:

Calories	564.1
Fat	28.1g
Cholesterol	103.7mg
Sodium	1712.7mg
Carbohydrates	53.0g
Protein	26.4g

* Percent Daily Values are based on a 2,000 calorie diet.

SIMPLE CALIFORNIA STYLE PANINI

Ingredients

- 2 avocados, halved and sliced
- 1/3 C. sun-dried tomato, smoked, julienned
- 2 tbsp red onions, diced
- 2 C. Baby Spinach, lightly packed
- 16 oz. ciabatta rolls, split in half

Directions

- Set your panini press to medium as suggested by the manual.
- Place the avocado slices onto the bottom half of each roll, followed by the tomatoes, onion, and spinach.
- Place the sandwiches into the panini press and cook for about 4 minutes.
- Enjoy warm.

Servings Per Recipe: 4

Timing Information:

Preparation	30 mins
Total Time	30 mins

Nutritional Information:

Calories	177.8
Fat	14.9g
Cholesterol	0.0mg
Sodium	113.2mg
Carbohydrates	12.0g
Protein	3.1g

* Percent Daily Values are based on a 2,000 calorie diet.

ROAST BEEF AND PASTRAMI PANINI WITH HOMEMADE THOUSAND ISLAND DRESSING

Ingredients

Dressing

- 3/4 C. mayonnaise
- 1/4 C. sour cream
- 3/4 C. ketchup
- 1 tsp dill relish
- 1 tsp sweet pickle relish
- 1 tsp dried onion flakes
- 1/4 tsp garlic powder
- 1/2 tsp lemon juice
- 1/2 tsp balsamic vinegar
- 3 -4 Tabasco sauce
- ground black pepper

Sandwich

- 8 slices sourdough sandwich bread
- 4 oz. thousand island dressing
- 4 oz. aioli
- 8 slices muenster cheese, sliced
- 8 oz. rare roast beef, sliced
- 8 oz. pastrami, sliced
- dill pickle, as desired
- 4 oz. caramelized onions
- unsalted butter, melted

Directions

- Set your panini press as suggested by the manual.
- For the dressing: in a bowl, add all the ingredients and stir until blended nicely. Place the dressing onto 4 bread slices evenly.
- Place the aioli onto another bread slices evenly, followed by the Muenster cheese, roast beef, pastrami, pickles and caramelized onions. Cover with the remaining bead slices, dressing side down.
- Coat the outsides of each sandwich with the butter generously.
- Place the sandwich into the panini press and cook until golden brown. Enjoy hot.

Servings Per Recipe: 4

Timing Information:

Preparation	15 mins
Total Time	35 mins

Nutritional Information:

Calories	717.8
Fat	39.4g
Cholesterol	150.8mg
Sodium	1916.9mg
Carbohydrates	46.0g
Protein	46.0g

* Percent Daily Values are based on a 2,000 calorie diet.

SEATTLE TUNA PANINI

Ingredients

Bean Spread

- 1 (15 1/2 oz.) cans garbanzo beans, drained
- 2 cloves garlic
- 1/4 C. of mint
- 2 tsp lemon zest
- 3 tbsp lemon juice
- 3 tbsp extra-virgin olive oil
- 1/4 tsp salt
- 1/4 tsp ground black pepper

Sandwich

- 1 C. pitted black olives, chopped
- 2/3 C. extra-virgin olive oil
- 1/2 tsp salt
- 1/2 tsp ground black pepper
- 2 (5 1/2 oz.) cans Italian tuna in olive oil, drained
- 1 (13 3/4 oz.) cans quartered artichoke hearts, drained
- 8 small baguette, sliced lengthwise
- 2 C. arugula

Directions

- For the garbanzo bean spread: in a blender, add all the ingredients and pulse until smooth.
- Place the spread into a bowl and keep aside.
- For the sandwich: in a bowl, add the tuna, artichokes, olives, oil, salt and pepper and mix well.
- Place the bean spread onto both baguettes halves evenly.
- Place the tuna mixture onto the bottom half of each baguette, followed by the arugula.
- Cover with the top halves of the baguettes bread and enjoy.

Servings Per Recipe: 6

Timing Information:

Preparation	20 mins
Total Time	20 mins

Nutritional Information:

Calories	1691.4
Fat	54.4g
Cholesterol	33.7mg
Sodium	3660.0mg
Carbohydrates	229.5g
Protein	69.8g

* Percent Daily Values are based on a 2,000 calorie diet.

Topped Banana Panini

Ingredients

- 3 ripe bananas, sliced
- 12 slices whole wheat bread
- 1 C. chocolate hazelnut spread
- 16 tbsp unsalted butter, softened
- 3 tbsp confectioners' sugar

Directions

- Set your grill for medium-high heat and lightly, grease the grill grate.
- In a bowl, add the bananas and mash until smooth.
- Arrange the bread slices onto a platter.
- Place the mashed banana onto 6 bread slices and cover with the remaining slices.
- Place the butter onto both sides of each sandwich.
- Cook the sandwiches onto the grill until golden brown from both sides.
- Remove the sandwiches from the grill and dust with the confectioners' sugar.
- Enjoy hot.

Servings Per Recipe: 6

Timing Information:

Preparation	10 mins
Total Time	20 mins

Nutritional Information:

Calories	744.2
Fat	47.9g
Cholesterol	81.4mg
Sodium	320.1mg
Carbohydrates	73.9g
Protein	9.0g

* Percent Daily Values are based on a 2,000 calorie diet.

Sonoma Pesto Vegetable Panini

Ingredients

Panini

- 1/4 C. olive oil
- 2 small Japanese eggplants, sliced crosswise
- 2 zucchini, sliced crosswise
- 1 small red onion, sliced
- salt & ground black pepper
- 2 French baguettes
- 1/2 C. basil pesto
- 8 oz. water-packed mozzarella cheese, drained, sliced
- 2 tomatoes, sliced
- 1/2 C. roasted red pepper
- 8 large basil leaves

Pesto

- 2 C. basil leaves
- 1/4 C. toasted pine nuts
- 2 garlic cloves, peeled
- 1/2 tsp salt
- 1/4 tsp ground black pepper
- 1/3 C. about extra virgin olive oil
- 1/2 C. grated Parmesan cheese

Directions

- In a bowl, add the zucchini, eggplant, onion slices, oil, salt and pepper and toss to coat well.
- Place a grill pan over medium-high heat until heated through.
- Place the vegetables slices in batches and cook for about 8 minutes, flipping once half way through.
- Transfer the vegetables onto a platter and keep aside to cool completely.
- Cut each baguette into 6 equal sized pieces and then, cut each in half.
- Place the pesto onto both sides of all the bread pieces.

- Place the eggplant slices onto the bottom halves of the bread pieces, followed by the zucchini, onion, tomato, mozzarella and roasted pepper.
- Season with the salt and pepper lightly and cover with the top halves of bread pieces.
- For the pesto: in a food processor, add all the ingredients except the oil and cheese and pulse until finely chopped.
- While motor is running, slowly add the oil and pulse until smooth.
- Transfer the pesto into a bowl and stir in the cheese.
- Enjoy the sandwiches alongside the pesto.

Servings Per Recipe: 12

Timing Information:

Preparation	30 mins
Total Time	40 mins

Nutritional Information:

Calories	434.5
Fat	20.5g
Cholesterol	18.6mg
Sodium	827.0mg
Carbohydrates	49.5g
Protein	14.9g

* Percent Daily Values are based on a 2,000 calorie diet.

PROVOLONE TURKEY PANINI WITH CRANBERRY DIP

Ingredients

Dip

- 1 (12 oz.) cans cranberry sauce
- 1 C. orange juice
- 1 C. ginger ale
- 2 tbsp light brown sugar
- 1/4 tsp salt

Panini

- 12 slices whole wheat bread
- 2 lb. roasted turkey breast, shaved
- 6 oz. provolone cheese

Directions

- For the dip: in a pot, add all the ingredients and cook until boiling.
- Set the heat to low and cook for about 22-25 minutes.
- Meanwhile, for the sandwiches: set your panini press as suggested by the manual.
- Place the turkey onto 6 bread slices, followed by the cheese.
- Cover with the remaining bread slices.
- Place the sandwich into the panini press and cook until golden brown.
- Enjoy warm alongside the dip.

Servings Per Recipe: 6

Timing Information:

Preparation	5 mins
Total Time	30 mins

Nutritional Information:

Calories	610.0
Fat	20.6g
Cholesterol	117.8mg
Sodium	751.0mg
Carbohydrates	60.8g
Protein	46.1g

* Percent Daily Values are based on a 2,000 calorie diet.

Balsamic Chicken Cutlet Panini

Ingredients

- 1 lb. chicken cutlet
- salt
- pepper
- 1 1/2 tbsp thyme, chopped, divided
- 6 tbsp olive oil, divided
- 2 garlic cloves, chopped
- 3 tbsp balsamic vinegar
- 4 sandwich buns, split
- 1/2 red onion, sliced
- 1 bunch arugula

Directions

- Season the chicken with 1 tbsp of the thyme, salt and pepper.
- In a skillet, add 2 tbsp of the oil over medium-high heat and cook until heated through.
- Add the chicken and cook for about 6-10 minutes, flipping once half way through.
- With a slotted spoon, place the chicken onto a plate.
- In the same skillet, add the remaining oil over medium-high heat and cook until heated through.
- Add the garlic and sauté for about 20 seconds.
- Add the remaining thyme and vinegar and cook for about 20 seconds.
- Add the cooked chicken and cook for about 2 minute, tossing frequently.
- Remove from the heat.
- Arrange the bottom halves of sandwich rolls onto a platter, followed by the chicken, onion, arugula and pan sauce.
- Cover with the top half of the rolls and enjoy.

Servings Per Recipe: 4

Timing Information:

Preparation	10 mins
Total Time	20 mins

Nutritional Information:

Calories	432.2
Fat	23.5g
Cholesterol	65.8mg
Sodium	280.8mg
Carbohydrates	23.2g
Protein	30.5g

* Percent Daily Values are based on a 2,000 calorie diet.

Moroccan Chickpeas Panini

Ingredients

- 3/4 C. canned chickpeas, drained
- 2 tbsp lemon juice
- 1 tbsp water
- 2 tsp capers
- 2 tsp olive oil
- 2 garlic cloves, minced
- 4 C. torn spinach
- 1/4 tsp salt
- 1/8 tsp black pepper
- 2 (2 1/2 oz.) submarine sandwich bread, halved horizontally
- 2 large plum tomatoes, sliced

Directions

- In a blender, add the chickpeas, capers, lemon juice and water and pulse until smooth.
- In a nonstick skillet, add the oil over medium-high heat and cook until heated through.
- Add the garlic and stir fry for about 1 minute.
- Add the spinach and cook for about 3 minutes.
- Stir in the salt and pepper and remove from the heat.
- Set your panini press as suggested by the manual.
- Place the chickpeas mixture onto the bottom half of each roll, followed by the spinach and tomato slices.
- Cover with the top half of each roll.
- Place the sandwich into the panini press and cook for about 2-3 minutes.
- Enjoy warm.

Servings Per Recipe: 2

Timing Information:

Preparation	10 mins
Total Time	15 mins

Nutritional Information:

Calories	181.1
Fat	5.9g
Cholesterol	0.0mg
Sodium	695.3mg
Carbohydrates	27.5g
Protein	7.0g

* Percent Daily Values are based on a 2,000 calorie diet.

1960's Fruit Panini with Shakes

Ingredients

- 6 large egg yolks
- 1/2 C. sugar
- 2 C. milk
- 1 C. heavy cream
- 2 vanilla beans, split and seeds scraped
- 1 lb. strawberry, sliced
- 1/2 C. orange juice
- 1 tsp grated orange zest
- 1 tbsp balsamic vinegar
- salt & ground black pepper
- 8 slices brioche bread
- 1/2 C. mascarpone
- 2 tbsp unsalted butter, softened
- 2 pints strawberry ice cream

Directions

- In a metal bowl, set a strainer and then, arrange the bowl in another metal bowl of ice water.
- In a bowl, add 1/4 C. of the sugar and egg yolks and beat until slightly pale.
- In a pot, add the cream, milk and vanilla beans with the seeds and cook until just starts to boil.
- Remove from the heat and slowly, add the hot milk into the egg mixture, beating continuously until well combined.
- Add the milk mixture into the pot over medium heat and cook for about 4-5 minutes, mixing continuously.
- Remove from the heat and place the milk sauce into the bowl with the strainer.
- Keep aside to cool completely, stirring often.
- Meanwhile, in another pot, add the remaining 1/4 C. of the sugar, strawberries, orange zest, orange juice, vinegar, salt and pepper over medium-high heat and cook until boiling.
- Cook for about 10 minutes, mixing frequently.

- Remove from the heat and place the jam into a bowl.
- Keep aside to cool completely.
- Set your panini press as suggested by the manual.
- Place the mascarpone onto 4 brioche slices evenly.
- Place the jam onto remaining bread slices evenly.
- Arrange the slices together to make sandwiches.
- Coat the outsides of each sandwich with the butter evenly.
- Place the sandwiches into the panini press and cook for about 5 minutes.
- Place the sandwiches onto a platter and dust with confectioner's sugar.
- Cut each sandwich in half.
- In a food processor, add the milk sauce and ice cream and pulse until smooth.
- Transfer the milkshake into serving glasses.
- Enjoy the sandwiches alongside the shake.

Servings Per Recipe: 4

Timing Information:

Preparation	30 mins
Total Time	2 hrs.

Nutritional Information:

Calories	1365.4
Fat	56.5g
Cholesterol	466.8mg
Sodium	1394.0mg
Carbohydrates	185.5g
Protein	32.1g

* Percent Daily Values are based on a 2,000 calorie diet.

VEGETARIAN BURGER PANINI

Ingredients

- 1 C. boiling water
- 8 pieces sun-dried tomatoes
- 4 morning star farms spicy black bean veggie burgers
- 1/4 C. light mayonnaise
- 1/4 C. seafood cocktail sauce
- 4 tsp prepared horseradish
- 8 slices sourdough bread
- nonstick cooking spray
- 1/4 C. banana pepper ring, drained
- 1/4 C. chopped red onion

Directions

- Set your panini press as suggested by the manual.
- In bowl, soak the sun dried tomatoes in boiling water for about 5 minutes.
- Drain the dun dried tomatoes well and ten, chop them finely.
- Meanwhile, prepared the black bean burger as suggested on the package.
- In another bowl, add the cocktail sauce, mayonnaise, horseradish and chopped tomatoes and mix well.
- Coat the bread slices with the cooking spray evenly.
- Arrange 4 bread slices onto a platter, greased side down.
- Place the mayonnaise mixture evenly, followed by the pepper rings and onion.
- Cover with the remaining bread slices, greased side up.
- Place the sandwiches into the panini press and cook until golden brown.
- Cut each sandwich in half and enjoy.

Servings Per Recipe: 4

Timing Information:

Preparation	15 mins
Total Time	30 mins

Nutritional Information:

Calories	192.8
Fat	9.5g
Cholesterol	8.7mg
Sodium	620.5mg
Carbohydrates	15.4g
Protein	11.9g

* Percent Daily Values are based on a 2,000 calorie diet.

APPENDIX I: OILS, SPREADS, SPICE MIXES

FRENCH TAPENADE SPREAD

Ingredients

- 2 C. pitted oil-cured black olives
- 3 tbsp drained capers
- 3 tbsp extra virgin olive oil
- 2 tbsp lemon juice
- 2 cloves garlic
- 2 tsp thyme

Directions

- In a blender, add all the ingredients and process until well combined.
- Enjoy the tapenade onto your favorite sandwiches.

Servings Per Recipe: 4

Timing Information:

Preparation	4 mins
Total Time	5 mins

Nutritional Information:

Calories	172.8
Fat	17.3g
Cholesterol	0.0mg
Sodium	777.7mg
Carbohydrates	5.7g
Protein	0.8g

* Percent Daily Values are based on a 2,000 calorie diet.

HERBS DE PROVENCE SPICE MIX

This is a spice mix popular in southern France. It is great in veggie stews and as a dry rub for grilled meats. This spice provides a very unique taste that is characteristic of France.

Ingredients

- 2 tbsps dried rosemary
- 1 tbsp fennel seed
- 2 tbsps dried savory
- 2 tbsps dried thyme
- 2 tbsps dried basil
- 2 tbsps dried marjoram
- 2 tbsps dried lavender flowers
- 2 tbsps dried Italian parsley
- 1 tbsp dried oregano
- 1 tbsp dried tarragon
- 1 tsp bay powder (finely ground bay leaves)

Directions

- With a mortar and pestle grind fennel seed and rosemary. Then combine with bay powder, savory, fennel, thyme, rosemary, basil, parsley, marjoram, oregano, lavender, and tarragon in a bowl.
- Then transfer to an appropriate container for storage.

Timing Information:

Preparation	Cooking	Total Time
5 m		5 m

Nutritional Information:

Calories	2 kcal
Fat	0 g
Carbohydrates	0.3g
Protein	0.1 g
Cholesterol	0 mg
Sodium	1 mg

* Percent Daily Values are based on a 2,000 calorie diet.

Flavored Garlic Oil Drizzle

Ingredients

- 1 C. canola oil, or olive oil
- 6 -8 garlic cloves, crushed

Directions

- In a heavy-bottomed pot, add the oil over medium-low heat and cook until heated through.
- Add the garlic and cook until browned, stirring frequently.
- Remove from the heat and keep aside to cool completely.
- With a strainer, strain the oil into a bowl, discarding the solids.
- Transfer the oil into an airtight container and store in fridge.
- Coat your favorite panini sandwiches with the garlic oil before cooking.

Servings Per Recipe: 1

Timing Information:

Preparation	2 mins
Total Time	32 mins

Nutritional Information:

Calories	244.2
Fat	27.2g
Cholesterol	0.0mg
Sodium	0.3mg
Carbohydrates	0.7g
Protein	0.1g

* Percent Daily Values are based on a 2,000 calorie diet.

THANKS FOR READING! JOIN THE CLUB AND KEEP ON COOKING WITH 6 MORE COOKBOOKS....

http://bit.ly/1TdrStv

 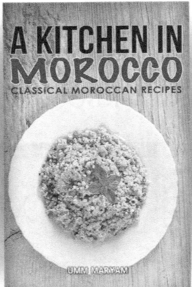 

To grab the box sets simply follow the link mentioned above, or tap one of book covers.

This will take you to a page where you can simply enter your email address and a PDF version of the box sets will be emailed to you.

Hope you are ready for some serious cooking!

http://bit.ly/1TdrStv

Come On...
Let's Be Friends :)

We adore our readers and love connecting with them socially.

Like BookSumo on Facebook and let's get social!

Facebook

And also check out the BookSumo Cooking Blog.

Food Lover Blog

Made in the USA
Middletown, DE
09 June 2019